LIBERAL EUROPE

1 *The Drummer Boy's Dream* by F.J. Shields (1866): militarism in an age of sentimentality.

LIBERAL EUROPE

THE AGE OF BOURGEOIS REALISM 1848–1875

W.E. MOSSE

with 73 illustrations, 9 in colour

THAMES AND HUDSON · LONDON

Picture research by Alla Weaver

© 1974 THAMES AND HUDSON LTD, LONDON

Printed and bound in Great Britain by Jarrold and Sons Ltd, Norwich

ISBN 0 500 32032 2 hardcover
ISBN 0 500 33032 8 paperback

CONTENTS

2 *Iron and coal* by William Bell Scott (1861): sketch for mural at Wallington Hall, Northumberland. A heroic view of industry as seen from the point of view of the successful industrialist. Not only industrial achievement but also the advance of political freedom is represented. The newspaper reports Garibaldi's victory at Caserta.

The period of European history covered by the present volume – though productive of great and lasting achievements – was distinguished neither by the originality of its thought nor by the refinement of its culture. Both were essentially derivative, though the age was marked by the appearance of two influential works, Darwin's *Origin of Species* and the first volume of *Das Kapital*. Perhaps significantly, no single 'ism' – not even liberalism, the representative ideology of the age – adequately covers the bulk of its numerous manifestations.

In the realm of ideas this was primarily an age of pragmatism, of diffusion and of popularization. In its culture, similarly, it was characterized by a spirit of eclecticism. As for its major preoccupations, these, like its achievements, were predominantly of a practical and material nature. They were concerned on the one hand with industry, commerce, communications, technology and, to some degree, science, on the other with politics, diplomacy, armaments and war. Such interests, moreover, were an accurate reflection of the actual direction of European civilization in a period of growing industrialization, urbanization and the growth of capitalist relationships, as well as the political reconstruction of the European continent and the increasing militarization of public life.

These developments, though they affected every part of Europe to a greater or lesser extent, were, however, spread unevenly. In fact they were concentrated mainly in the leading industrial nations, Great Britain, France and Germany (as well as the United States of America). And just as a study of the *ancien régime* in Europe will be concerned primarily with the society, institutions and ideologies of France, so, in the present case, it is appropriate to focus attention on Great Britain, then the recognized 'pace-setter' of European industrial civilization. In the realm of military affairs, on the other hand, it is France and Germany (Prussia) which hold the centre of the stage. Compared with these leaders in the arts of industry, finance and war, predominantly pre-industrial states like the Habsburg monarchy, Russia or

Italy play a relatively minor role. So, in a different sphere, do the 'masses', whether peasant, working-class or petty bourgeois. Their contribution to the industrial civilization of the age was either negligible or confined at best to the narrowly economic sphere. Rather, it was bourgeois élites, economic and intellectual, which helped to fashion the civilization and establish the values of industrial society.

Representatives of rising industrialism did not find a clean slate. Nearly everywhere, they had to reach accommodations with entrenched pre-industrial groups, aristocratic, landowning or bureaucratic. In fact, diplomatic and military affairs as well as important areas of administration remained in most countries the safe preserve of these groups. Frequently, they determined also the patterns of social life. Over large areas of Europe, therefore, it is the interaction (and partial interpenetration) of aristocratic-traditional and bourgeois-commercial élites that provides the principal dialectic of the age. No single generalization about an entity as complex, diverse and unevenly developed as mid-nineteenth-century Europe can claim a general validity. Nor, given the necessary limitations of space, is it possible to do full justice to the many local or exceptional situations. All that can be attempted is to elucidate a number of features which give to European civilization of the period its distinctive character, differentiating it both from what went before and from what was to follow.

The author gratefully acknowledges his obligation to Drs Stephen Wilson and Richard Shannon, and Messrs David Barrass and Morley Cooper for valuable criticism and suggestions, and also to the general editor of the series for beneficial stylistic revisions.

3 Title-page device of *Le Génie Industriel*, a periodical devoted to inventors and inventions: the glorification of inventive genius.

I PORTRAIT OF AN AGE

Perhaps the outstanding characteristic of Europe in the years between the Great Exhibition of 1851 and the proclamation of the German Empire at Versailles in 1871 was a widely diffused feeling of hopefulness based on conspicuous material progress in many spheres. The thirties and forties, decades over-all of traditional scarcity overshadowed by Malthusian pessimism, had been marked by desperate social protest among the poor and by conscience-stricken questioning and widespread moral unease among the educated in the face of advancing industrialism – witness the bitter social commentary of Balzac, Dickens or Daumier, the anxious preoccupations of Proudhon, of Marx and Engels, of Thomas Carlyle and the young Disraeli. The eighties and nineties, again, marked by the social involvement of the founders of the Salvation Army, William and Catherine Booth, of the sociologist Charles Booth, the Fabians and Cardinal Manning, by the popularity of Zola's stark accusing naturalism and the doctrines of the German academic socialists, were a time when the undiluted capitalist ethic was once again called in question.

In the intervening decades – some critical voices notwithstanding – the majority of people appeared to be adjusting successfully to the conditions of urban and industrial life. There was a widespread confidence, reflected in, for instance, the optimistic philosophy of Herbert Spencer, in man's ability to master the forces of both nature and society. Such confidence drew apparent justification also from an unwonted degree of apparent (though to some extent relative) social stability. What, in a remarkable study of mid-Victorian England, has been termed 'the age of equipoise' describes, if with marked local variations, an essentially European phenomenon. In a similar manner, Asa Briggs's description of the mid-Victorian era as 'a great plateau bounded on either side by deep ravines and dangerous precipices' can be broadly applied to large areas of European life. A number of distinctive features taken in conjunction – widespread acceptance of industrialism and adaptation to its results, conspicuous material

9

progress accompanied by a relative sense of security and confidence (at times verging on complacency) together with a general acceptance of reality, the 'here and now' – give the age of prosperity its distinctive flavour.

The basis of this widespread confidence and dynamic optimism was, in the first place, economic. The years between 1849 and 1873 constitute a well-defined (moderately inflationary) 'trend period' of rising wholesale prices and fairly widely distributed prosperity, sandwiched between two 'trend periods' marked by falling wholesale prices and relative economic stagnation. To contemporaries, recalling the thirties and 'hungry forties', this was, by comparison, a time of real prosperity. The following generation, looking back from the vantage point of the 'Great Depression', would view the fifties and sixties as truly a 'golden age'. In each of these assessments, there was in fact an element of subjectivity; the actual prosperity of the age often was, and easily can be, exaggerated. Yet there is much evidence that in objective terms this was a period of rapid economic growth and of rising living standards for many, perhaps the majority.

This prosperity in its turn helped to colour intellectual attitudes. Even though cultural pessimism by no means disappeared, the age intervening between the philosophies of Byron and Malthus on the one hand and those of Wagnerian *Götterdämmerung* on the other was essentially optimistic in its positivist evolutionary philosophy. People found warrant, not only in present experience but in much of their thinking about it, for the belief in an ultimately happy outcome resulting from the steady over-all amelioration of the human condition. The essentially pessimistic philosophy of Christianity – most relevant to conditions of scarcity and deprivation – seemed to many to be losing at least some of its appropriateness. Prosperity instead gave an added impetus to the rival intellectual tradition of the Enlightenment, of Saint-Simon, Comte and the Utilitarians.

Corresponding attitudes appeared in the realm of culture. Here Romanticism, essentially the posture of escape (whether into the past, the inner self, the geographically remote and esoteric, 'nature' or simply into the imagination), was steadily yielding ground to Realism, with its attitudes of acceptance and analysis. Scientific – or would-be scientific – modes of thought achieved a degree of ascendancy also in the cultural sphere. Even when not actively promoting experiment and innovation, they stimulated accurate observation,

4 The golden age of the *bourgeois conquérant*, stranger to doubt and self-criticism, shines forth from this painting by F. Bazille (detail, 1868).

faithful representation and careful attention to detail. This in itself came close to a revolution in style, dethroning both Romanticism and the pervasive classical tradition. Yet Realism never gained an un-challenged ascendancy. Instead, it co-existed not only with belated remnants of the Romantic movement and residual elements of Neoclassicism but also with the first manifestations of a new Romanti-cism, the harbingers of Symbolism, *fin de siècle* decadence and Art Nouveau. No homogeneous or harmonious style could develop from such heterogeneous elements. Eclecticism, in the end, remained the dominant cultural aspect of the 'inter-Romantic' age.

Both Realism and eclecticism reflect, in essence, the cultural tastes of a bourgeoisie at a particular – ascending – stage in its evolution. Indeed the *bourgeois conquérant*, to use Charles Morazé's phrase, can be seen, at least in the more advanced industrial countries, not only as the period's patron and arbiter of taste, but more broadly as its most significant social type. 'May death find me on my feet, like so many men of the strong generation to which I belong', wrote Haussmann, in this as in much else a quintessential representative of the dynamic middle class. It was indeed a 'strong generation', and in certain respects an iconoclastic one, which not only left its mark on numerous manifestations of the age of prosperity but which collectively made the 'conquering bourgeoisie' the most significant class, although not by itself the dominant class of the age.

The term 'bourgeoisie' as employed in the present context should not be understood in the Marxist sense of describing as a social class the owners of the means of production. Instead, it is used to designate broadly strata of urban society (the question of the possible existence of a rural bourgeoisie is, at least for the moment, irrelevant), placed between traditional ruling élites (landowning or bureaucratic) on the one hand and the popular masses (primarily peasantry and urban proletariat but also including, at least for the present purpose, the petty bourgeoisie) on the other.

Within the bourgeoisie thus defined it is possible to distinguish several separate strata. Its leading élite, aptly described by the French term *la haute bourgeoisie* or *la grande bourgeoisie* (more precise in meaning than the Anglo-Saxon 'upper middle class'), consisted of bankers and merchants, financiers, ship- and mine-owners and wealthy industrialists – in fact Marx's class of property-owners and capitalists. This was a group which everywhere constituted a numerically insignificant fraction of the total population. In Britain, for example, the most advanced industrial nation, its number in 1871 may not have exceeded 40,000 in a total population of some 26 million. These included 17,000 merchants and bankers, 1,700 ship-owners and an unspecified number of factory- and mine-owners.

To some extent associated with this capitalist élite were the bourgeois professions, covering a spectrum from lawyers and engineers through doctors, architects and journalists to scholars, writers and the more successful artists. These professional groups were not numerous either. Thus Britain, in 1871, had 3,500 barristers, 12,000 solicitors, 7,000 architects and 5,000 civil engineers. There were 15,000 doctors but only just over 2,000 'authors, editors and journalists'. All told, the two élites, commercial and professional, may in 1871 have numbered (without dependants) some 100,000, about one-third of 1 per cent of the total population.

5 Eyre Crowe's *Dinner Hour, Wigan*. While buildings in an industrial setting can be shown realistically, Labour is shown idealized, enlarged and purified.

To the two preceding groups should be added the growing but socially less significant class of *rentiers* or people living on unearned income. In France, for instance, they tended to be people of modest means drawing a livelihood from government bonds, but in wealthier Britain they were as often as not comfortably-off men and women benefiting from the capital accumulation of earlier generations.

Altogether in Britain in 1871 there were some 170,000 'persons of rank and property' without visible occupation. Including these, the upper stratum of the British bourgeoisie may, by the early 1870s, have numbered something like a quarter of a million.

This figure receives some confirmation from the income-tax assessments made in 1865–66 under Schedule D, covering profits from business, the professions and investment. Of a total of 200,000 assessments in excess of £300, 7,500 were in a 'top bracket' of £5,000 and over, a further 42,000 between £1,000 and £5,000. In terms of income, therefore, by an admittedly arbitrary definition, perhaps 50,000 people might be included in the *haute bourgeoisie*. There is some support for such a figure in the fact that there were, in 1871, 90,000 female cooks (including, of course, those employed in aristocratic households). If such was the anatomy of the *haute bourgeoisie* in the most advanced society of the day, analogous groups in progressively less developed countries, while similar in structure, would be proportionately smaller in numbers. Below this top stratum were larger middle-class groups – with shopkeepers, artisans and white-collar salaried staff perhaps the most important constituent elements. Nor were these groups numerically large. In Britain, for instance, in 1871 there were 100,000 'commercial clerks' and 'bank clerks'. Such groups as a rule were not very active in public affairs except in their role as urban voters.

The available evidence is insufficient to establish definitely that even in areas of rapid industrial growth the middle classes increased proportionately more than the total population (which in Britain grew from 20.9 million in 1850 to 26.2 million in 1870, in Germany during the same period from 35.4 to 40.9 million and in France from 35.8 million in 1851 to 36.1 million twenty years later). It is noteworthy, however, that in Britain the number of domestic servants rose from 900,000 in 1851 to 1,400,000 two decades later. In other words, more households were employing servants or some households were employing more servants or, most probably, both.

Since the barriers to social ascent were no longer rigid, the bourgeoisie, apart from its natural increase, could draw on a reservoir which, in many European countries, consisted mainly of better-off elements among the peasantry. In more heavily industrialized and peasant-deficient Britain, on the other hand, the new bourgeois was more likely to come from the ranks of the 'aristocracy of labour', the

6 Detail from *Dividend Day at the Bank* by G. E. Hicks. The *rentier* class, living on investment incomes, was growing in numbers to the extent of attracting the artist's attention.

2.5 million earning, in 1867, between twenty-eight and forty shillings a week. The growing (and not very numerous) professions on the whole recruited themselves from within the ranks of the middle class. One conspicuous avenue of advance was through the Churches, including the Roman Catholic, which offered a recognized road of social ascent for both peasant and small-town children. Religious educational establishments, whether Nonconformist, Anglican, Roman Catholic or Orthodox, provided much of the secondary – and sometimes higher – education of future professional men. A second source of recruitment for the bourgeois intelligentsia was the business classes. The offspring of businessmen who failed to make good would often seek professional careers; so also would the descendants in the second or third generation of the most successful factory-owners and entrepreneurs. The numbers involved, however, were relatively small, particularly at the 'cultural' end of the professional spectrum.

Active social and political relations with members of the older ruling élites were confined to the highest strata of the bourgeoisie. These, a rising social group, were pressing both for increased social recognition and for a greater share of political power. The adaptation of the aristocratic, landowning élites to these pressures constitutes one of the most distinctive social and political phenomena of the period. The gradual interpenetration of aristocratic and *haut bourgeois* elements, combined with the relative acquiescence of the 'lower orders' during a period of rising living standards, produced the short-lived social equipoise characteristic of the age of prosperity.

In one respect the age could be seen as the culminating point of a social movement which went back to the French Revolution. In France, the process by this time was virtually complete with the unchallenged ascendancy, at any rate since 1830, of the *haute bourgeoisie*, as the lament of an Austrian diplomat in 1853 shows. In other countries, wrote Baron Hübner, where everything had not yet been levelled by sixty years of revolution as it had in France, there were still, thank God, separate classes. In France, on the contrary, money was everything and, in the sentiments of the nation, the Rothschilds and the Foulds had precedence over the Montmorencys and the Rohans.

Within a generation, as the age of prosperity drew to a close, Hübner's laments would be echoed by Anthony Trollope and Delane of *The Times* in Britain, by the historian Jacob Burckhardt and the novelist Friedrich Spielhagen in the German-speaking lands, and by the journalist Suvorin in Russia. In fact, such lamentations were exaggerated. While plutocracy undeniably advanced, aristocracies remained clearly recognizable everywhere. Secure in the deference of their social 'inferiors' they retained (even in France) many personal privileges and considerable influence in public affairs – besides in many cases replenishing their coffers, often by highly 'bourgeois' means. In fact, social developments in most countries during the period – and this was among its distinguishing features – favoured a *connubium* of the two groups, with aristocrats tentatively admitting, with more or less good grace, selected representatives of the upper bourgeoisie, either by marriage alliances or otherwise, into the charmed circle of hereditary privilege on a footing of near-equality. The cream of the bourgeoisie, for its part, battled with might and main to gain admission to the aristocratic sanctum, by buying landed estates with the obligatory 'hunting, shooting and fishing', aping aristocratic manners and mannerisms, and, above all, by acquiring titles whether by purchase, patent or marriage. Above all, the sons and even daughters of the wealthy were brought up as 'gentlemen' and 'ladies' in company with the scions of the aristocracy, in *lycées* or Jesuit colleges, in public schools, cadet corps or *Burschenchaften*. What was common to most countries, notwithstanding important local peculiarities, was the admission into the ruling élites of selected members of the bourgeoisie in gradually increasing numbers.

The social ascent of the bourgeoisie was accompanied, particularly during the sixties, by significant political gains. After the revolutionary 'flash in the pan' of 1848, lower chambers of parliament came to an increasing extent to be dominated by bourgeois parliamentarians: lawyers, manufacturers, bankers, journalists and, on occasion, professors. Legislation – sometimes by its very absence – tended increasingly to reflect their economic interests and needs. It was impossible, the aged Palmerston observed in 1864, to 'go on adding to the Statute Book *ad infinitum*'. This was the expression of sound bourgeois principles. In effect, the liberal doctrine of *laissez-faire* and of reducing to a minimum the role of government in economic affairs formed the kernel of the legislative philosophy of bourgeois political ascent.

Outside the economic sphere, except for the French bourgeoisie, historically older than the rest and turned, with victory, 'prematurely' conservative, bourgeois politicians remained on the whole reformist, sometimes radical. They adhered to a middle-class liberalism finely poised between monarchic-bureaucratic power or 'feudal' conservatism on the one hand, mass democracy on the other. Of the two, however, the former (on occasion in alliance with the latter) was normally the chief obstacle to the realization of bourgeois political aspirations. Broadly, with the monarchic and aristocratic systems weakening and with mass democracy still in its infancy, the age of 'equipoise' was also the 'golden age' of liberal parliamentarism and constitutional monarchy.

Yet the growing parliamentary influence of bourgeois politicians was reflected only imperfectly in the composition of governments. Except for France, whose 'mature' bourgeoisie had enjoyed political power since 1830, and, to a limited extent, the new kingdom of Italy, commoners either achieved real influence in government only towards the end of the period (Austria–Hungary 1867, Britain 1868) or never succeeded in doing so at all (Prussia–Germany and Russia). Though some monarchs and ministers developed bourgeois tastes and interests (Louis-Philippe, Prince Albert and Queen Victoria, Cavour) and though *grands seigneurs* of the old school were becoming something of a rarity, senior military, diplomatic and sometimes administrative posts remained the preserve of the old ruling classes. Aristocratic influence, firmly entrenched in important branches of government, remained preponderant. Nowhere was this more spectacularly the case than in the field of foreign policy, which in the age of the new diplomacy of 'blood and iron' remained wholly outside the grasp of bourgeois politicians. It was aristocrats almost exclusively who for traditional, largely dynastic ends manipulated the widespread nationalist passions of the age. The combination of dynastic direction with the wide prevalence of nationalist emotion did much to give international relations their distinctive flavour. This explains at least in part the seeming paradox that the age of prosperity and internationalist ideology was nevertheless also an age of widespread warfare. At the beginning of the period, Europe had been at peace for over a generation. After its end, it would be so once more. Between 1854 and 1871, however, five wars were fought, in which every major European power was involved at least once. If the American Civil War is added, there was peace in only six out of the seventeen years.

Prosperity contributed to war by removing financial inhibitions. Industrial techniques applied to the manufacture of armaments improved – on occasion decisively – the chances of military success. There was, moreover, a profound ambivalence in bourgeois-liberal ideology itself, committed as it was on the one hand to internationalism and free trade, on the other to crusading 'liberating missions', and prone to extreme nationalist passions. Above all, the wars of the age reflected a basic dualism, with an essentially internationalist and pacific commercial system interacting with, and also serving, a diplomatic-military system that was dynastic, aristocratic and not unwarlike. It was the non-bourgeois policy-makers who harnessed popular-nationalist fervour and progressive industrial technology to the attainment of their essentially old-fashioned objectives.

The legacy of the age was in the end like its character, ambivalent. It left, in most of the Continent, the groundwork of a bourgeois-

7 An engraving from the Leipzig *Illustrierte Zeitung* of 8 July 1871 shows triumphal junketings in Berlin after victory over France. An exuberant nationalism often overruled liberal internationalism in bourgeois hearts.

industrial civilization, but at the same time it produced a subtle militarization of life in some of the major countries, together with latent social conflicts and an exuberant nationalism which collectively paved the way for the subsequent age of imperialism. Thus the twin features of the age, prosperity and war, account in the main for its distinctive contribution to European history.

8 *The Railway Station* (Paddington) by W.P. Frith (*c.* 1862). While the main interest is the human scene in the foreground, the artist is also excited by the visual possibilities of the new industrial scene. Both the architect who designed Paddington Station and the artist who painted it wished to romanticize the railway, and the shapes are intended to be aesthetic as well as merely functional.

II THE ECONOMICS OF
PROSPERITY

About the turn of the nineteenth century, the economic life of Europe received a sudden impetus. In 1848, with the Continent in the throes of political upheaval, a different but possibly more profound revolution was initiated in distant California. John Augustus Sutter, while constructing a mill–dam, struck gold. By 1849, the great Gold Rush, celebrated in song, was under way. Two years later, prospectors again found gold, this time in faraway Australia. Following these discoveries, gold began to pour into bullion- and credit-starved Europe. Between 1852 and 1860 gold exported from the state of Victoria, the leading Australian producer, was valued at £95 million (rated at a uniform eighty shillings per ounce). Within a decade, the bullion reserves of the leading industrial countries had risen by a third. From 1850 to 1873, the average annual increase in the world's stock of monetary gold was about 4 per cent.

Among the consequences of the inflow was an unprecedented expansion of the European banking system and, with it, of bank investment in industry and commerce. In France, already the home of the wealthiest branch of the Rothschild family, new credit institutions, including the Crédit Foncier and Crédit Mobilier (1852), Société Générale de Crédit Industriel et Commerciel (1859), and the Crédit Lyonnais (1863) were founded in rapid succession. Of particular importance were the Crédit Mobilier, the great investment bank set up by Napoleon III's régime to provide capital for commercial and industrial ventures, and the Crédit Lyonnais, which combined the role of a modern deposit bank (largely for small savers) with that of a highly speculative investment institution. The value of Crédit Mobilier shares increased fourfold within the space of a few years.

Similar banking growth also took place east of the Rhine. Here the outstanding new banks were the Bank für Handel und Industrie in Darmstadt (1853), the Kreditanstalt für Handel und Gewerbe, founded by the Vienna Rothschilds in 1855, and the Discontogesellschaft (1856). The latter part of the period saw the rise on the European continent of

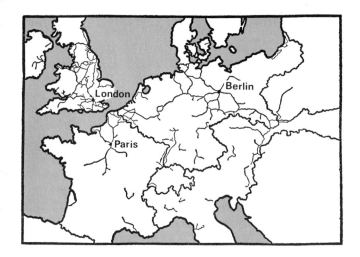

9, 10 The railways of Europe, 1848 and (*opposite*) 1878 – a striking expansion. The greater density of lines in England, where railway construction began, and Belgium, is noticeable.

the great specialist *banques d'affaires* or investment banks, Société Générale pour favoriser le Développement du Commerce et de l'Industrie en France (1864), Deutsche Bank (1864), Dresdner Bank (1872) and Banque de Paris et des Pays Bas (1872). All over western and central Europe, and as far afield as Russia, the funds of private investors mobilized through credit banks were being channelled by means of flotations and loans into industrial and commercial enterprises. The financial infrastructure was being created for the accelerated capitalist development of European industry. Prominent among the influences promoting the mobilization of savings and the development of financial institutions had been a widespread railway boom, creating a demand for a better articulated and more generalized credit system.

Some of the new investment was speculative and unsound. The ill-effects of this, however, were mitigated, at least in part, by the adoption of the joint-stock principle. British legislation between 1856 and 1862 pioneered the concept of limited liability. France (1867) and Germany (1870) followed suit. No longer need would-be investors fear the fate of the British Member of Parliament who, having invested £50 in a company, found himself liable for a debt of £50,000. Despite failures and bankruptcies, joint-stock companies contributed effectively to industrial development. As the biographer of a Rhenish industrialist noted in retrospect, they had developed in modern society 'with the energy and speed of a force of nature', and had become 'a striking feature of the present time'. In response to conditions in Europe and America, joint-stock companies had arisen simultaneously in all states which had 'assumed the great task of material progress', and in the course of a few decades had material creations to their credit 'before which even the great works of antiquity and the Middle Ages must bow'.

The bulk of the capital attracted by banks and joint-stock companies during the fifties and sixties flowed into communications, particularly into railway construction. Between 1850 and 1870, Europe's rail network expanded from 14,000 to 65,000 miles, that of North America from 9,000 to 56,000. In Europe in 1848, only England and Belgium had even the rudiments of a national railway system. Thirty years later (with England and Belgium still leading) the whole of Europe was covered by a network of varying density. About one-sixth of the world's future track had been laid, the most important sixth according to at least one authority.

Hardly less striking was the progress being made in navigation. Steamships, thanks to numerous improvements made from the middle of the century onwards, became safer, speedier and more economical. Steam navigation, hitherto confined to short-haul freight traffic, came into increasing use for more distant voyages and for the transportation of bulky goods. Whereas in 1850 Europe's steam registration amounted to a mere 186,000 tons net, by 1870 it had reached almost 1.5 million.

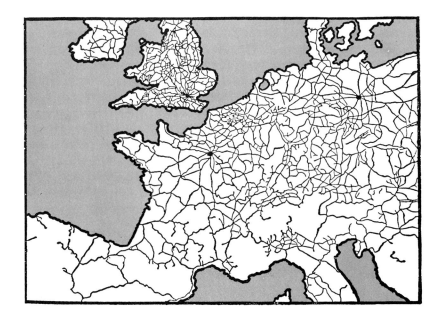

Steamship and locomotive, together with cable and telegraph, revolutionized communications. As early as 1850 railway fares in Britain were less than two-fifths of those formerly charged by coaches. Travel time had been reduced by two-thirds. Between 1850 and 1855, journeys between London and Edinburgh were shortened by four hours and between London and the south-west from nine hours to just over seven. Steamships more than halved the sailing time of even the speediest packet, besides reducing dependence on wind and weather. At the same time, domestic and international telegraph services accelerated world-wide communications. In 1851, a cable from Calais to Dover created the first of many links between Britain and the Continent. In 1866, following several unsuccessful attempts, the first transatlantic cable was finally installed. Cables reached Calcutta in 1870 and Australia in 1871. The Universal Postal Union, set up in 1874, standardized international postal practices. A world-wide network of communications was thus emerging, and with it a marked expansion of international trade and the rudiments of a world economy.

The building of railways and steamers, together with the growing use of iron in engineering and construction work and also for armaments, was the basis for the prosperity and rapid expansion of European metallurgy (as well as of the ancillary coal-mining industry). The combined iron output of Britain, France and Germany rose from about 2.75 million tons in 1851 to 8.5 million in 1870. Moreover, following Bessemer's invention of a new method for purifying pig-iron, the production of steel (hitherto almost a semi-precious metal) at moderate prices became a commercial possibility. Between 1856 and 1870 the output of British steel increased sixfold and its price was almost halved. Steel in the sixties was being put to a variety of new uses (boiler-making, machine tools, arms, locomotives, ships, rails). A steadily growing demand for iron and steel products made the fortunes of several enterprises, prominent among them Krupps in Essen, Whitworth and Armstrong in the north of England, the integrated Cockerill works at Seraing in Belgium, and Schneider at Le Creusot. Le Creusot, from an overgrown village of 8,000 in 1851, grew within fifteen years to a town of 24,000, with Schneider alone employing some 10,000 workers. The work-force of Krupps in Essen grew from 2,000 in 1861 to 4,000 in 1863 and 6,000 the following year. Order books everywhere reflected a seemingly insatiable demand for rails, locomotives, wheels, axles, propellers, ships and machinery of every kind. The widespread demand (including extensive orders for both consumer and capital goods from Australia, California and the rapidly advancing North American frontier) made this a period of rising wholesale prices. Indeed, under the impact of the inflow of overseas bullion, Europe had at first experienced a bout of rapid price inflation. A sharp though short-lived economic recession in 1857 had somewhat checked the trend and prices thereafter had levelled off, with wholesale prices some 25 per cent, retail prices about 13 per cent, above those of 1850.

Rising wholesale prices coincided with significant technological advances. Some of these were in the industrial field. Thus the cost of steel was cut by the discovery of new smelting techniques (Bessemer 1856, Siemens-Martin 1856–64). Werner Siemens, father of the modern electrical industry, designed for use in telegraphy the armature which bears his name. His invention of the dynamo in 1867 was followed six years later by the construction of the first model capable of prolonged operation. Important new machine tools were designed (the universal milling machine in 1861, the automatic lathe *c.* 1870). William Perkin in 1856 extracted mauve dye from coal-tar, making a significant contribution to industrial chemistry. In 1867, Nobel took out his British patent for dynamite. Six years later, Mond invented a process for the extraction of soda.

By this time, oil and rubber were coming into industrial use (the first oil-well in Pennsylvania was drilled in 1859). Aluminium, then a rare precious metal, was admired at the Court of Napoleon III. Considerable progress was made in photography and in the construction of the bicycle. The Yale lock dates from 1855, more ominously the machine-gun from 1861. A domestic and social transformation was initiated when Singer in 1851 began the mass production of his sewing-machine (20,000 machines were turned out in 1863) – opportunely for Levi Strauss, a young immigrant from Bavaria, who was devising and producing, for the benefit of Californian gold-miners, the garment soon to be known as 'levis'. Though a number of these inventions had to await the last quarter of the century for their full industrial and commercial exploitation, they nevertheless contributed, not least psychologically, to the industrial buoyancy of the period. A boundless future of industrial and technological progress appeared to be opening before mankind. Even the wildest fantasies of Jules

Verne's widely read science-fiction stories (*Five Weeks in a Balloon* 1863, *Journey to the Centre of the Earth* 1864, *From the Earth to the Moon* 1865, *The English at the North Pole* 1866, *Twenty Thousand Leagues Under the Sea* 1870, the immortal *Around the World in Eighty Days* 1873) no longer appeared beyond the bounds of possibility.

Economic growth based on a growing demand for industrial products, on technological advance and on rising wholesale prices benefited the majority of those engaged in industry and trade. For the industrialist, profits often sufficed to finance expansion, while except in times of recession, credit and loan capital were readily available. The steady wage-earner also shared modestly in the relative prosperity. In Great Britain, for instance, while average real wages remained almost stationary during the fifties (with money wages, though rising, lagging behind soaring retail prices), they rose by about 40 per cent between 1862 and 1875. For those who were able to push up their wages faster than the rise in prices, this meant, in E. J. Hobsbawm's words:

> unstinted food, clothes of the same pattern as the middle class, when house rents permit, a tidy parlour, with stiff, cheap furniture which, if not itself luxurious or beautiful, is a symptom of the luxury of self-respect, and an earnest of better things to come, a newspaper, a club, an occasional holiday, perhaps a musical instrument.

In a revealing passage, an old Chartist returning to Lancashire in 1870 noted:

> My sorrowful impressions were confirmed. In our old Chartist time, it is true, Lancashire working men were in rags by the thousands; and many of them often lacked food. But their intelligence was demonstrated wherever you went. You would see them in groups discussing the great doctrines of political justice. . . . *Now* you will see no such groups in Lancashire. But you will hear well-dressed working men talking, as they walk with their hands in their pockets, of 'Co-ops' and their shares in them or in building societies. And you will see others, like idiots, leading small greyhound dogs.

Clearly, the slow *embourgeoisement* of at any rate the top layer of the British 'manual labour class' was an accompaniment of industrial prosperity. Even the lowest-paid labourers, earning ten to twelve shillings a week (almost half the total number), were experiencing a modest improvement in their situation. True there was, as yet, no significant decline in the death-rate (including that of infants). On the other hand, evidence suggests that wage-earners were consuming increasing quantities of meat, fats, sugar and beer, as well as imported produce like tea, cocoa and rice. In Britain, the per capita consumption of sugar, for example, trebled in the thirty years after 1840. By 1870, it had reached almost a pound per week. Nor were such improvements in living standards confined to Britain. In Germany, the average annual wage of the Saar miner rose from 386 marks in 1850 to 634 in 1860 and 729 in 1869. Similarly, the daily wage of a Krupp metal-worker rose from 1.25 marks in 1850 to 2.06 in 1860 and 2.86 in 1869. The wage of an unskilled day-labourer was estimated in 1858 by the Cologne Chamber of Commerce to have risen in the preceding decade between 20 and 30 per cent. In France the increase of real wages between 1860 and 1870 has been calculated at 18 per cent.

Nor were the economic benefits of the period confined to those who engaged in industrial or commercial pursuits. Agriculture, which still provided a livelihood for the bulk of Europe's populations, also received a stimulus. One major factor contributing to its new-found prosperity was the growth of markets for its produce. From 1830 to 1870 the total number of consumers increased in Great Britain by almost a third, in western Europe (excluding France) by a quarter. The growth of towns,★ the widespread rise in purchasing power and living standards, as well as a mounting industrial consumption pro-duced a growing demand for agricultural products. One result was a rise in prices. Between 1850 and 1873 the price of wool in Europe went up by nearly three-quarters, while in Britain it doubled within the space of twenty-five years; the prices of meat and dairy produce increased by between a quarter and a half. Though the price of cereals grew less sharply, rising yields per acre (with an increased acreage) made these also a profitable crop. The new railways meanwhile increasingly provided a convenient means for the transportation of agricultural produce. Massive overseas competition would not make itself felt until the seventies.

Large landowners (and, especially in England, their tenants) benefited most from agricultural prosperity. In Germany, for example, large estates east of the Elbe produced profitably for the market increasing quantities of grain, livestock and wool. Farming here was becoming more heavily capitalized. An active land-market developed,

27

★ The population of London, for instance, rose from 2.3 million to almost 3.8 million between 1850 and 1880, that of Paris from 1 million to 2.2 million. Berlin during the same period grew from 420,000 to 1 million, Vienna from less than 450,000 to over 700,000.

as wealthy commoners in growing numbers acquired aristocratic estates (*Rittergüter*). Peasant farming also could be profitable, particularly in the vicinity of urban centres, with their increasing demand for vegetables, eggs, milk, cheese and meat. Rural credit at reasonable rates was becoming more readily available. In Germany, the first of the co-operative Raiffeisen banks for the provision of rural credit was set up in 1862. In France, too, rural credit was improved. Whereas peasant farming there had stagnated in the fifties, thereafter it began to show signs of improvement under the impact of rail transportation and better credit facilities. Better farm implements were employed more widely and the use of fertilizers spread. Wheat began to replace rye or buckwheat as the peasant's staple diet. Wine increasingly became an article of common consumption. In general, not only the peasant's lot but even that of the humble farm-labourer improved somewhat – notably in Britain, thanks to the relative scarcity of rural labour resulting from migration to the towns. Though by no means everyone employed on the land benefited, the period was still, in broad terms, an age of farming prosperity.

The economic causes generating the prosperity of the age were reproduced broadly, though in varying degrees, in every major country of Europe and North America. Moreover, different regions were increasingly drawn together by railway and steamship, cable, post and telegraph, as well as by the international mobility of investment capital. A further unifying factor was the widespread adoption of free-trade principles and, to a lesser extent, free-trade policies. For reasons of enlightened self-interest, Great Britain had led the way. Others, in this as in other respects, tended to follow the British lead. The late fifties and early sixties in particular were marked by a series of international trade agreements providing for tariff reductions. Aided by these policies, international trade grew apace. According to one calculation the value of international exchanges rose by 40 per cent in the thirties and again in the forties, by 80 per cent during the fifties (with the figure somewhat inflated by the higher wholesale prices) and by another 50 per cent in the course of the following decade. It was an expansion shared by every major industrial nation.

If, however, the prosperity of the fifties and sixties was widely shared, there was no doubt who was the chief beneficiary. Great Britain, it has been said, was 'the world's workshop, the world's shipbuilder, the world's carrier, the world's banker and the world's clearing house'. The

11 The Royal Commissioners for the Exhibition of 1851, painted by H. W. Phillips. Prince Albert is in the chair, with Lord Derby on his left and Paxton leaning on the table. Between the Prince and Paxton is Lord John Russell, the Prime Minister; behind Lord Derby are Sir Robert Peel and Robert Stephenson.

gold discoveries, wrote *The Times* in 1851, had given 'an electric impulse to our entire business world'. So also had the Great International Exhibition, the first of its kind, of the same year. The history of the world, exulted one of the Exhibition's promoters, recorded 'no event comparable, in its promotion of human industry'. A great people had 'invited all civilized nations to a festival to bring into comparison the works of human skill'. Or, as another commentator remarked, 'for the *first* time in the world's history, the men of Arts, Science and Commerce were permitted by their respective governments to meet together to discuss and promote those objects for which civilized nations exist.'

In all, there were more than thirteen thousand exhibits, drawn from every corner of the globe. Machinery predominated. American exhibits, for instance, included a sewing-machine, a pioneer McCormick reaper, and 'a most luxuriously fitted plough', those from Europe textile machinery from Oldham and De la Rue's envelope machine. Joseph Whitworth's precision machine tools were highly commended.

A visitor sensitive to the great movements of the age might have paused more particularly in front of four exhibits. One was a nugget of gold from California, much admired by the crowds. '*Auri sacra fames*', wrote a contemporary. 'What no motive, human or divine, could effect, springs into life at the display of a few pellets of gold in the hands of a wanderer. This may be God's chosen way to fulfil his commandment and "replenish the earth".' Another notable exhibit was the electric telegraph, which enabled no less a personage than the Queen herself to address greetings to her loyal subjects in Edinburgh and Manchester. Yet a further significant exhibit, admired by experts of every nation, was a cast-steel ingot displayed by Krupps, weighing 4,300 lb., the like of which had never been seen before. Finally, 'the crowning glory of Prussian industry', Krupps also exhibited 'the much discussed Krupp gun of cast-steel with its mahogany carriage'. The gun, standing under the canopy of a Prussian military tent and with half a dozen Krupp-manufactured cuirasses – highly polished – piled at its base, was a favourite exhibit, especially with the ladies, who considered it 'delightful'. Indeed, though Krupp would have to wait another eight years for the first orders for his guns, ingot and gun in conjunction established on solid foundations the world-wide reputation of the Essen firm. Its fame, thus linked to the opening of the era, would, twenty years later, contribute not a little to the beginning of its decline.

Yet, though the Krupp exhibits were indeed spectacular, and though, as official publicity proclaimed, the Exhibition was dedicated to 'the Works of Industry of all Nations', once again one nation excelled. The choice of London as the venue for the first exhibition of its kind was far from accidental. At least half the total space had been occupied by the products of Great Britain and her colonies. Indeed, what was being presented to the world was nothing so much as a picture of British industrial supremacy. Not surprisingly, the Exhibition provoked an outburst of exuberant British self-confidence. The tone of the country was right, the *Manchester Guardian* rejoiced complacently in its end-of-year review, and it was set on the road to boundless progress.

Nor was such confidence misplaced. Britain, enjoying a head start over her rivals, was to maintain her industrial and commercial lead in most fields down to the end of the period. She continued to produce roughly half the world's pig-iron (2.25 million tons out of 4.47 million in 1850, 5.96 million out of 12.26 million twenty years later). For the world-wide railway boom, she supplied everything from navvies to engineers and from rails to railway engines. Of Europe's total steam registration of 186,000 tons net in 1850, 168,000 were British. In 1870 the figures were 1,483,000 and 1,113,000 respectively. Again, in the five years after 1848, British exports rose by almost two-thirds. Commodity exports between 1850 and 1860 jumped by 90 per cent, by another 60 per cent in the succeeding decade. Invisible exports more than balanced soaring imports. Until the early fifties favourable British trade balances had averaged around £7 million a year; by the late sixties, they were approaching £40 million. In the hectic five years after 1868, that figure almost doubled. British overseas investments meanwhile rose from some £100 million in 1830 to £700 million in 1870.

Though Britain maintained a virtually unchallenged over-all commercial and industrial lead, France was achieving a rate of economic growth that was scarcely less impressive. Napoleon III, partly under Saint-Simonian inspiration, was determined to develop the country's economic resources. In ringing tones, he outlined his economic programme in a celebrated speech at Bordeaux in 1852: 'We have immense uncultivated areas to reclaim, roads to open, harbours to dig, rivers to make navigable, canals to finish, our railway network to complete. . . . We have to bring our great western ports nearer to the American continent by accelerating the communications we still lack.' In the years which followed, the French government set in motion a great programme of public works (usually self-financing). New canals were constructed, millions of acres of wasteland reclaimed. The bulk of major trunk lines was completed. Marseilles was transformed into a busy modern port, a leading emporium of the Mediterranean. The Messageries Maritimes (founded in 1851) showed the French flag on the oceans of the world. In 1855, the Péreire brothers set up the Compagnie Générale Maritime, destined to play a notable part in the development of the port of Le Havre. Trade was developed with the Americas and the Far East.

The effect of these and other developments on French commerce and industry was electrifying. Between 1851 and 1870 the combined value of French imports and exports nearly trebled. Indeed, it is an eloquent commentary on French economic progress that possibly no less than 44 per cent of the new gold from overseas found its way ultimately into French coffers. There was a growing demand for machinery of every kind. New techniques, significantly named *le système anglais*, were introduced in the metallurgical industries. Between 1850 and 1860 production and consumption of coal, coke and steel roughly doubled. Between 1850 and 1870 the output of iron rose from 400,000 to 1,180,000 tons. In 1862, *The Economist*, commenting on the economic progress of France since 1852, noted that 'wherever the traveller strays, he sees the reign of growth and prosperity. Whatever town he enters, he sees new symptoms of progress and of hope, whatever district he visits he finds some trace of the same pervading and omnipresent spirit. In the capital, the change is not only considerable but wonderful.'

Indeed, under the energetic direction of Haussmann, Prefect of the Seine département, the face of Paris was being transformed. For seventeen years, until his dismissal in 1869, he toiled indefatigably, in collaboration with the Emperor, to transform the overcrowded and insanitary city inherited from the Valois and Bourbons into the modern Paris of broad boulevards, spacious squares and fine parks admired by the world ever since. Almost 30,000 old houses were demolished (earning Haussmann, from one of his numerous critics, the title of 'Attila of expropriation'), over 100,000 others either rebuilt or reconstructed. New buildings included landmarks like Les Halles and the Opéra. Seventy miles of new road were laid, over four hundred miles of pavement constructed, transport facilities modernized. Drainage, water supply and cemeteries were radically improved, inaugurating a new era of better hygiene for the city. Thanks to this, to migration from the provinces and to incorporations, its population almost doubled between 1851 and 1872 (from about 1 million to 1.8 million).

Perhaps the apotheosis of Haussmann's new Paris and indeed of the new spirit of French enterprise was the great international Industrial Exhibition of 1867. Twelve years before, in 1855, the Empire had made its industrial début with another International Exhibition. Then, there had been 24,000 exhibitors; now their number was almost doubled. Whereas in 1855 attention had centred on electrical appliances, gas heating, rubber for industrial uses, and photography, it now focused on railway equipment and on industrial items like coal-cutting equipment and gas and compressed-air machinery. Krupp in 1855 had exhibited an ingot of his celebrated cast steel weighing 10,000 lb. and a field-gun with a steel barrel some 50 lb. lighter than the bronze ones in use in the French army. Twelve years later, with a monumental lack of imagination, he displayed both a mammoth steel ingot weighing 80,000 lb. and, more ominously, a giant thousand-pounder 14-

12, 13 Baron Haussmann, Prefect of the Seine and architect of the modern Paris, presents his plans to the Emperor Napoleon III (*right*). In the 1860 bird's-eye view below, the city we know today can be seen taking shape. In the foreground is the Arc de Triomphe, vertically above it in the middle distance the Tuileries and the Louvre.

inch siege-gun, 'a monster such as the world has never seen'. The King of Prussia, together with the Tsar the star visitor to the Exhibition – twelve years earlier it had been Queen Victoria – contemplated the gun with amazement. In general, British judges at the Exhibition commented, not without concern, on the 'wonderful display' of foreign machinery and woollen goods. And many of these goods were French, a vivid testimony to French industrial progress since 1855.

France's greatest technological marvel, however, and the one that most stirred the imagination of contemporaries, was not on show at the Exhibition. Nine years before, in 1858, Ferdinand de Lesseps had floated his Suez Canal Company. In 1869, the Canal was officially opened amid universal acclamation. One American commentator described it as one of 'the two greatest constructive works that have ever been undertaken', the other being the Pacific Railroad. The Canal cut the distance from Europe to the East by over a third (the journey from London to Bombay, for instance, was reduced from 10,700 miles to 6,300). Moreover, the successful cutting of the Isthmus was accompanied by significant technological innovation. Under the direction of Voisin Bey, first engineer-in-chief, and his assistant Laroche, the muscle power of some 30,000 Egyptian fellaheen was progressively replaced by machinery of 10,000 h.p. capable of moving two million cubic metres of soil a month. Powerful trough dredgers, designed and constructed by Lavalley, a French contractor, together with other machinery, eventually enabled the company to dispense with three-quarters of its original labour force. Indeed, the quality of French technology was now such as to cause serious concern in Great Britain. As early as 1864, a British engineer had lamented the fact that Schneider was not only supplying locomotive engines, iron plates and forgings to customers who 'used to come to us for these commodities', but was even importing locomotives into England. Recently, a major order for iron in a foreign country had gone to France despite a slightly lower British tender, because the customer 'could more perfectly rely on the uniform excellence of the quality of iron from Creusot than from England'.

Nor was France now the only potential threat to British industrial supremacy. The Prussian artillery tests for heavy naval guns held in 1868 pitted Armstrong's nine-inch gun against Krupp's ninety-six-pounder. The final triumph of the latter, which broke Armstrong's long-standing near-monopoly in the field of naval ordnance, marked the ending of an era. In fact German industry, notwithstanding distracting political preoccupations, had been making gigantic strides. The stagnation of the years 1848–50, a German contemporary noted, had ended after the fall of the French Republic. The totally depleted warehouses had had to be filled again and when at the same time the effects of the introduction of Californian gold and the low discount rate made themselves felt by way of England, 'there gradually developed a spirit of enterprise more powerful than any experienced in Germany up to that time'.

The steamboat traffic on the rivers, the shipment of goods on the railroads, the construction of ships and machinery grew at an extraordinary rate. Railroads and machine shops, coal mines and iron-foundries, spinneries and rolling mills seemed to spring out of the ground, and especially in the industrial regions of Saxony, the Rhineland and Westphalia, smokestacks sprouted from the earth like mushrooms.

Following a depression in the late fifties, economic progress was resumed. Iron production, a mere 215,000 tons in 1850, had reached 1.4 million by 1870. While at mid-century German iron output had been little over half that of France, by 1870 it had overtaken it (1.4 million tons against 1.1 million). German production of iron in that year was not much behind that of the USA (*c.* 1.7 million tons), though even American, German and French output combined still fell below the British total of almost 6 million tons. In the industrial sphere at least, Germany had overtaken France, though the latter remained financially the stronger. Significantly, Krupp's order book now included names like Whitworth, Blakely and Armstrong (the last with an order for 112 guns).

Both the general industrial advance of the period and the relative progress of France, and even more of Germany, are illustrated by approximate comparative figures★ for the capacity of all steam-engines ('000 horsepower):

	1850	1860	1870	1880
Great Britain	1,290	2,450	4,040	7,600
Germany	260	850	2,480	5,120
France	270	1,120	1,850	3,070

★ Quoted in W. Minchinton, 'Patterns of Demand, 1750–1914' in C. M. Cipolla (ed.), *The Industrial Revolution* (London 1973), p. 165

14, 15 Krupps of Essen, the great German steel and armaments works, in 1852 a moderate-sized plant in a rural setting (*above, left*), by 1873 (*right*) a vast industrial complex.

The economic growth of the period was not confined to the major industrial nations. Elsewhere too, industry was developing, though on a more modest scale. In Russia, for example, the output of coal rose from nearly 18 million *pud* (62 *pud* equal 1 ton) in 1860 to over 70 million in 1873 and to 200 million by the end of the decade (iron, on the other hand, was still largely imported). Russia's railways grew from some 1,000 miles in 1860 to over 11,000 in 1874. According to an estimate made by Lenin, the product of thirty-four branches of Russian industry, worth 200 million roubles in 1864, increased to 350 million in 1873 and to 500 million by the end of the decade. Even remote agricultural countries like Russia were being drawn, if slowly and selectively, into the general industrial movement of the age.

Though the age in general was one of relative prosperity, the progress of industrialization and capitalism did not bring improved conditions for all. Prominent among the victims – particularly in Germany – were sizeable groups of artisans, particularly the less adaptable. In many parts of Europe, the slow agony of surviving hand-loom weavers, locked in unequal competition with power-driven machinery, continued. Among rural populations, traditional subsistence farmers on marginal land or remote from urban centres normally lacked capital, skill and enterprise to benefit from new opportunities. By no means all who moved into the new industrial centres proved capable of adapting to conditions of urban living and factory work. Chronic ill-health and sickness, physical and mental,

were rampant, as were alcoholism, disease and physical deformity. Some could find only casual employment, while others had to work in sweat-shops or at one of the marginal trades described graphically in Henry Mayhew's *London Labour and the London Poor* (1861–62). 'Those that cannot work and those that will not work', in Mayhew's words, often depended for their very survival on the vagaries and caprices of private charity.

The economic ill-effects of the industrial system were not confined to the poor alone. At a very different level the entrepreneur – and this did not exclude even a firm like Krupps – might find himself short of working capital and, in conditions of severe competition, at the mercy of the business cycle. Crises like those of 1857, 1866–67 or 1873 remorselessly claimed their victims. So did a variety of (sometimes fraudulent) speculative ventures, attracting the gullible from all walks of life by the promise of rapid gain.

Yet, if industrial progress spelt ruin even for some members of the bourgeoisie, it opened up to others unprecedented opportunities, especially to men with little (often borrowed) capital. What counted was neither birth nor education, but drive, determination, a readiness to take risks, some engineering or business acumen and a degree of luck. In Germany, a relatively late entrant into the industrial field, the new entrepreneurs were recruited from a variety of social strata. Some engine-builders of the fifties had started their careers as skilled crafts-men. Alfred Krupp, scion of an ancient merchant family of Essen, had had to leave school at the age of fourteen on the death of his father, who had brought his foundry to the verge of bankruptcy. It then employed seven workmen. Equally, however, the new 'captains of industry' might be the sons of army officers, clergymen, or wealthy

37

merchants. Leading bankers and merchants included among their number, besides representatives of old patrician families, the progeny of bailiffs, clergymen, thread-manufacturers, merchants and grocery dealers. As for the professional men who provided much of the intellectual leadership of the German bourgeoisie, as often as not they were the offspring of clergymen, private employees or petty officials. In general, this was a society where, with economic expansion and with the parallel expansion of the army and the bureaucracy, careers were open to talent – at any rate within the broad spectrum of the middle classes.

Opportunity was also the keynote in the Paris of Napoleon III and Baron Haussmann. It was of several kinds. One was speculation. Though many speculators fell by the wayside, some made colossal and rapid fortunes by the appreciation and fluctuations on the Bourse of shares, such as those of the Crédit Mobilier. (It is perhaps not without significance that gambling started in Monte Carlo in 1856.) Another source of profit was the demolition, property and construction boom connected with the rebuilding of Paris. By the mid-sixties, there had grown up a group of specialist demolition contractors, which included a fair number of 'cultivated gentlemen' who, instead of becoming lawyers or doctors, had gone into business in the hope of making a brilliant and rapid fortune. Such realists could now make commercial use even of their erudition. Being in contact with antique dealers and collectors they had to be able to 'tell a lock from the right period under the rust' and to recognize at a glance a Lancret, a Trémouillère or a Watteau. They had to know how to bring out the artistic value of a piece of marble or a piece of panelling.

Perhaps the greatest (if untypical) example of the successful building contractor was Joseph Thome, thirteenth child of a peasant in the Cévennes. In 1830, Thome had set out from his native village to seek employment as a navvy in Paris. With some borrowed money, he set up as an independent builder. During the forties, the scale of his operations increased, but it was the Empire which gave him his chance. Thome built sumptuous mansions first along the Champs-Elysées, later throughout the new quarter of the Etoile. When he died towards the end of the century, he left sixty million francs. Though Thome's career was a particularly striking case of opportunities seized, it was by no means unique. More than one young peasant, though unable to emulate a Thome, was, whether through commerce, state employ-

16 The Suez Canal, opened in 1869, was France's greatest technological achievement in the nineteenth century. It saw, among other things, the first large-scale use of earth-moving equipment.

ment or the Church, drawn into what Giovanni de Lampedusa, in his novel *The Leopard*, has described as 'that process of continual refining which, in the course of three generations, transforms innocent peasants into defenceless gentry'.

Though it cannot, of course, be proved by statistics, there is little doubt that this was in fact for many – and might well appear to more – an age of economic opportunity. In considerable numbers men of modest background were drawn into the thriving bourgeois order. Indeed, as early as 1859 (in the Preface to *A Contribution to the Critique of Political Economy*) Karl Marx had commented perceptively on 'the new stage of development upon which bourgeois society seemed to have entered with the discovery of gold in California and Australia'. Economic developments accentuated by the discoveries were, in varying degree, laying the foundations of industrial bourgeois society in the major European countries.

MAN·IS·BVT·A·WORM·

17 Charles Darwin gave a scientific foundation to current evolutionary theories; his views of man's descent were caricatured, not unkindly, in *Punch*.

III THE PHILOSOPHY OF PROSPERITY AND ITS CRITICS

The striking economic progress of the period exercised a profound influence upon its general attitudes. The philosophy of an age which prided itself on its concrete material achievements was essentially pragmatic and unspeculative. Though rooted in the thought of the French Enlightenment, it bore – especially in the vulgarized form in which it gained world-wide currency – the trademark 'made in England'. Indeed, in some respects, it resembled nothing so much as a rationalization of British industrial progress.

In general, the contribution of the mid-century generation to speculative thought was slight. Its achievement, rather, lay in the transformation of the *avant-garde* speculations of an earlier intellectual élite into a durable philosophy or world view adapted to the needs of the 'railway age'. Its assumptions about the evolution of society were optimistic. In essence, it was a bourgeois philosophy of progress – though spreading literacy, the slow secularization of education and the increase in semi-popular reading matter assisted its diffusion among other classes – based on the cult of science, invention and technology. The key terms in its vocabulary, terms which recur in the journalism, political speculation and politics of the age, were 'work' or 'labour', 'science', 'knowledge', 'progress' and 'civilization'. A characteristic statement of its credo occurs in a guide published by two French engineers, Droux and Rueff, in connection with the Paris Exhibition of 1867:

> World exhibitions are a part of that vast economic progress which includes railways, the electric telegraph, steam navigation, the piercing of isthmuses. . . . Whether called Crystal Palace, Palace of Industry or Palace of the Champ de Mars, the Exhibition is a temple raised to the glory of science and of labour; it is the opening of a new era. The past reserved its favour for great conquerors and raised statues for them in glorification of destructive genius; the future will reserve its triumphal arches and monuments for productive genius which is also the symbol of Peace.

More succinctly, de Lesseps expressed a similar philosophy when, in speaking of the building of the Suez Canal, he wrote that 'there was not a camel driver among us who did not consider himself an agent of civilization. That is why we succeeded.'

The same outlook was expounded, more flamboyantly, by Tupper:

> These twenty years – how full of gain to us,
> To common humble multitudinous Man;
> How swiftly Providence advances thus
> Our flag of progress flaming in the van!
> This double decade of the world's short span
> Is richer than two centuries of old,
> Richer in helps, advantages and pleasures,
> In all things richer – even down to gold.
> To all of every class in liberal measures:
> We travel quicker now than Isthmian might,
> In books we quaff the veriest Hebe's chalice;
> All wonders of the world gladden the sight
> In that world's wonder-house, the Crystal Palace;
> And everywhere is Might enslaved to Right.

The historian Henry Buckle, the first volume of whose *History of Civilization in England* appeared in 1857, in an attempt to define and systematize empirical advance in historical terms, committed himself to the proposition that 'the progress of every people is regulated by principles . . . as certain as those which govern the physical world'. Buckle's yardstick of progress was the growth of knowledge, which he sought to establish by induction from relevant historical material.

The social outlook reflected in statements such as these – the product of industrial and technological progress – was practical, optimistic, lacking in sophistication and more than a little complacent. At its core lay faith in the perpetuity and the inevitability of human progress, the pleasing assurance that, whatever its temporary setbacks, humanity would always resume its advance. While this, in the first place, was held to mean that increased production would make the world a more comfortable place for more of its inhabitants, it was tacitly assumed and, at times, explicitly stated, that such material progress was inseparably linked to moral advance. Science, invention and labour in combination would finally bring about a millennium based on abundance, happiness and moral perfection for all.

18 The skilled workers, joining together, sought not only to improve their physical well-being but also to find dignity. This device uses classical and Christian motifs to enhance the status of the skilled working man.

BE UNITED AND INDUSTRIOUS

AMALGAMATED SOCIETY OF ENGINEERS, MACHINISTS, MILLWRIGHTS, SMITHS, AND PATTERN MAKERS.

This is to Certify that   was admitted a Member of the
                    Branch on the   day of   18
In witness whereof we have subscribed our names and affixed the Society's Seal.

PRESIDENT.   SECRETARY.

L'Extinction du paupérisme was the significant Saint-Simonian title of one of Louis Napoleon's early political pamphlets. In essence, the philosophy it expressed did not differ widely from that being elaborated by Karl Marx (the first volume of whose *Das Kapital* appeared in 1867) and Friedrich Engels. For Marx also – however bitterly he might castigate the evils of capitalist industrial society – capitalism with its striking increases of production constituted, at any rate in a contemporary setting of residual feudalism, a wholly 'progressive' force. Marx and Engels, it is true, sought to combine this philosophy with a logically incompatible faith in revolution. But Marx's quarrel with the spokesmen of bourgeois ideology was neither about ends (universal plenty) nor yet about means (science, technology and invention) but about the more remote issue of distribution and social control once plenty had been achieved. In Marx's calmer moments, though the 'end game' might be different, the earlier stages would be played by roughly similar rules. Abundance through production and as a result, the flowering of human personality, creativity and happiness was his goal (though perhaps as a means to an end) no less than that of his rivals. Marx, moreover, like many among his contemporaries, linked material progress with moral regeneration. For him also, the future stood under the sign not only of man's inventiveness and ingenuity, but also of his moral perfection.

The moral aspects of material progress, the place of character and personality in worldly success, were matters of concern to thinking men and women. Prominent among publicists preoccupied with this aspect of industrial activity was Samuel Smiles, whose writings gained a wide popularity. Smiles, following medical school in Edinburgh and an apprenticeship in radical journalism, eventually settled down to life as a railway administrator. Early in his career, he had conceived an admiration for the strong, determined and ingenious men, the frequently self-taught pioneer inventors and industrialists, who had laid the foundations of British industrial supremacy. Being of a didactic and moralizing disposition, Smiles resolved to present these men to his contemporaries – above all to the growing ranks of literate mechanics – as models for emulation. What he particularly wished to show was the nature of the moral qualities which, after trials and tribulations, had brought his heroes industrial success. Smiles's first work, *The Life of George Stephenson* (1857), won its author instant recognition. Soon, researches among the papers of industrial pioneers

Das Kapital.

Kritik der politischen Oekonomie.

Von

Karl Marx.

Erster Band.

19 Karl Marx, Charles Darwin's 'sincere admirer' concerned with a different form of evolution, wished to dedicate to him the English translation of *Das Kapital* – a compliment politely declined.

supplemented by interviews, yielded three bulky volumes of *Lives of the Engineers* (1861–62). Their success proved that popular industrial biography had arrived. It was a sign of the times. Smiles's prosaic, moralizing and didactic accounts of the lives of industrial worthies marked a radical change in intellectual climate since the days of Jane Austen, Byron, Scott or indeed Dickens.

In the period between his life of Stephenson and those of the engineers Smiles produced the work which not only made his name a household word in every part of the globe but also established his reputation with posterity. *Self-Help* was an instant, indeed a sensational success. It sold 20,000 copies in 1859, the year of publication, 55,000 by 1864, three times that number within twenty-five years. *Self-Help* was translated into every major language and a large number of lesser ones besides (including Armenian, Siamese and several Indian languages). Numerous editions appeared in the United States where success literature, at this time, was much in vogue. Smiles acquired an enthusiastic following in Italy where, during a visit, he was received both by the Queen and by Garibaldi. On the walls of the Khedive of Egypt's palaces, extracts from *Self-Help* alternated with others from the Koran. Indeed, Smiles's philosophy was relevant wherever, with the break-up of traditional societies, individuals felt the urge to 'better themselves' in life. Drawing on the more profound thinking of his friend, mentor and fellow Scotsman Thomas Carlyle (to whom he also owed the title of his work), Smiles provided some-

45

thing of a moral foundation for the widely diffused philosophy of material progress. His was a capitalist entrepreneurial ethic drawn largely from Calvinist sources and adapted to the needs of an emergent industrial society.

The key to the Smilesian ethic is found in the gospel of work. 'An endless significance', Carlyle had written, 'lies in work; properly speaking, all true work is Religion.' Developing the theme, Smiles linked work not only with the well-being of the individual but also with that of society:

> As steady application to work is the healthiest training for every individual, so it is the best discipline of a state. Honourable industry travels the same road with duty, and Providence has closely linked both with happiness. The Gods, says the poet, have placed labour and toil on the way leading to the Elysian fields.

Work was for Smiles a moral categorical imperative:

> The necessity of labour may, indeed, be regarded as the main root and spring of all that we call progress in individuals and civilization in nations, and it is doubtful whether any heavier curse could be imposed on man than the complete gratification of all his wishes without effort on his part, leaving nothing for his hopes, desires or struggles. The feeling that life is destitute of any motive or necessity for action must be of all others the most distressing and insupportable to a rational being.

Smiles's 'Faustian' ethic, in effect, exalted less the material rewards of labour (though these also were not to be despised) than its character-forming qualities. The foundation of all 'true greatness of character' for Smiles lay in 'resolute determination in the pursuit of worthy objects'.

> Energy enables a man to force his way through irksome drudgery and dry details and carries him onward and upward in every station in life. It accomplishes more than genius, with not one half of the disappointment and peril. It is not eminent talent that is required to assure success in any pursuit so much as purpose – not merely the power to achieve but the will to labour energetically and persever-ingly. Hence energy of will may be defined to be the very central power of character in a man – in a word, it is the Man himself. It gives impulse to his every action, and soul to his every effort.

Work, for Smiles, was the foundation of character, and it was the formation of character – 'human nature in its best form . . . moral order embodied in the individual' – which was his major concern. With character, moreover, Smiles associated a host of the lesser bourgeois virtues: attention, application, accuracy, method, punctuality and despatch, the qualities required for the efficient conduct of business of any sort. Such qualities might, at first sight, appear to be small matters. They were nevertheless of essential importance to human happiness, well-being and usefulness. Moreover, character developed in this way fulfilled an important social function. Men of character not only constituted the conscience of society but in every well-governed state also its best motive power. It was moral qualities, in the main, which ruled the world.

Smiles thus delineated for the benefit of his contemporaries the positive 'ideal' type for a bourgeois-industrial society. Bourgeois morality in an entrepreneurial setting was linked to individual success and happiness. Bourgeois virtue received its bourgeois reward. The moral earnestness of Scottish Presbyterianism entered, in Smiles's teaching, into a dynamic partnership with the 'technocratic' ideal of the inventive and industrious mechanic. Here was a model for the young, a recipe for success in an industrial society. Nor was this a remote or abstract ideal. Dozens of instances cited in Smiles's writings bore witness to its eminently practical nature. Character, in Smiles's real-life 'success stories', actually had played the part ascribed to it and received its just reward. (Instances to the contrary, almost by definition, were excluded from Smiles's purview.)

The Smilesian ethic of diligence and reward was not confined to industrious mechanics. In a very similar spirit Anthony Trollope, probably the most successful English writer of the age, in his autobiography ascribed much of his success to persistence. This quality, he complacently noted, had enabled him to exceed the literary output of any other living English author. In making this boast about the quantity of his output, Trollope added, he did not claim any literary excellence. What he did lay claim to, however, was 'whatever merit should be accorded to me for persevering diligence in my profession'. He made this claim not with a view to his own glory, but for the benefit of those who might read these pages when young and might intend to follow the same career. '*Nulla dies sine lineâ*. Let that be their motto.' And let their work be to them as was his to the common labourer. There was no need for Herculean effort. He himself had never been a slave to his work. But he had been constant, 'and constancy in labour will conquer all difficulties. *Gutta cavat lapidem non vi, sed saepe cadendo.*' It was thus he had, in the last twenty years, made something near £70,000 by literature alone, a result 'comfortable but not splendid'.

Smiles himself had indignantly denied the charge that he was preaching a gospel of vulgar success. Certainly in his scale of values mere wealth, though often the reward of bourgeois virtue, took second place to the qualities of character and will of which it was the outward reflection. Smiles's appeal, in fact, was directed to ambition rather than love of luxury, comfort or ostentation. For him, the accomplishment of a moral duty took precedence over enjoyment – though it was held to contain happiness within itself. Indeed, the Smilesian ethic was surrounded with an aura of hard work and austerity recalling its Presbyterian origins. Smiles's was a secularized (already partly obsolescent) gospel for the successful (first-generation) entrepreneur. Directed to the individual, it based on the competition of individuals the well-being of society. It was, at the same time, a voluntarist philosophy. The individual held in his hands the key to his own fate. By the application of the appropriate moral qualities he could achieve worldly success – as indeed, in theory at least, could any other member of society. In no small degree, the wide appeal of Smiles's doctrine lay in this voluntarism. For Smiles, a field-marshal's baton lay concealed in the knapsack of every soldier of industry. The underlying implications of his philosophy supported a qualified optimism. Though not everyone would be successful, it was open to each individual to succeed by his own efforts. Indeed, in its implied assumption of substantial opportunities for all – Smiles for this reason was a prominent advocate of compulsory elementary education – the doctrine contained elements of complacency, if not wishful thinking. Moreover, Smiles assumed that the successful striving of its members assured the well-being of society, in both its material and moral aspects. Though success could not be guaranteed either for the individual or for society, both were vouchsafed at least the prospect of achievement through the application of appropriate moral virtues.

The want of over-all certainty in Smiles's ethic was supplied by a different and complementary doctrine, the popularized theory of evolution commonly known as 'Darwinism'. If Smiles had expounded the ethical basis of prosperity, Charles Darwin unwittingly helped to provide its essential cosmology. It was a curious coincidence that *The Origin of Species* appeared in the same year as *Self-Help*. Its impact, like that of Smiles's work, was instantaneous. Everyone had read it, a contemporary noted, or, at any rate, had expressed an opinion on its merits or defects. Old women of both sexes considered it a dangerous book. Soon educated men and women everywhere were familiar with at any rate the outline of Darwin's theory. By 1872, *Atlantic Monthly* claimed, natural selection had 'quite won the day in Germany and England, and very nearly won it in America'. The American social reformer Charles Loring Brace considered Darwin's book 'one of the great intellectual events of the century, influencing every department of investigation'.

Yet evolution was hardly a new discovery. Evolutionary theories had been current in European intellectual circles for several generations. Charles Darwin's contribution to their diffusion was twofold. In the first place, by his painstaking observations of plant and animal life, Darwin provided a scientific inductive basis for what, until then, had been largely cosmological speculation. Thanks to his (and Alfred Russel Wallace's) contribution, theories of evolution passed, in Comte's terminology, from the philosophical to the scientific stage. The theory of evolution now became scientifically respectable, a fact which promoted its incorporation into the general world view of the age. Moreover, Darwin's controversial explanation of the mechanism of evolution by means of 'natural selection' added the concept of the 'struggle for existence' to its intellectual arsenal. This, in Spencer's formulation of the 'survival of the fittest', became the key to the explanation of a wide variety of phenomena well beyond the sphere of biology. As Walter Bagehot explained it, just as every great scientific conception tended to advance its boundaries and to contribute to the solution of problems not thought of when it was stated, so here 'what was put forward for mere animal history' might 'with a change of form, but an identical essence, be applied to human history'.

The theory of evolution, as legitimized by Darwin, was soon found serviceable for the interpretation of a wide variety of social phenomena. Evolution, for many, became the basis of a coherent, dynamic, secular world view. In particular, the associated ideas of the 'struggle for existence' and the 'survival of the fittest' rapidly established themselves as the dominant ideas of the age. Accidentally (that is, both unintentionally and almost certainly unaware of the wider implications of his theory) Darwin had made the crucial contribution to its general world view. Though 'Darwinism' was modestly and scrupulously disowned by its originator, it became the central core of a world-wide philosophy. Nor was this accidental. The notions popularized in connection with Darwin's scientific findings satisfied the major intellectual needs of evolving bourgeois-capitalist society. Both Darwin and Wallace drew the concept of 'the struggle for existence' from Malthus's classic essay on population, which in turn was closely related to the doctrines of the classical economists. Thus it is hardly surprising that the new theory of evolution was found to be highly serviceable for the interpretation of bourgeois-capitalist society. In fact, not only did evolution meet the need for a scientific explanation (or model) of its social mechanics; at the same time it provided, as businessmen in particular were not slow to notice, 'scientific' justification for many of its practices.

Evolution could be readily identified with competition, for which, indeed, it appeared to provide a 'scientific' justification. By elevating competition to the status of a 'law of nature' – Smiles called it 'the great social law of God' – 'natural selection', the 'struggle for existence' and the 'survival of the fittest' seemingly legitimized the struggle of both individuals and groups in every sphere of human endeavour, not least the economic. No less an authority than John D. Rockefeller informed a group of schoolchildren that the growth of a large business was merely the survival of the fittest. The American Beauty rose, he added, could be produced in the splendour and fragrance which brought cheer to its beholder 'only by sacrificing the early buds which grow up around it'. It had been the same with the Standard Oil Company. Nor was this, in business affairs, an evil tendency but simply 'the working out of a law of nature and a law of God'. In fact, progress in the view of many was the product of what Macaulay called 'the tendency in every man to ameliorate his condition'. To numbers of its devotees, moreover, evolution appeared happily synonymous also with moral selection. It was not only the physically and professionally but also the 'morally' fittest who tended to survive. The successful man of affairs thus was authorized to consider himself the embodiment also of moral excellence.

In the social sphere the theory of evolution lent itself to profoundly optimistic interpretations. Using characteristically biological analogies, Herbert Spencer, the evolutionary 'apostle of North America' asserted as early as 1850 in his *Social Statics*:

> The ultimate development of the ideal man is logically certain – as certain as any conclusion in which we place the most implicit faith; for instance that all men will die. . . . Progress, therefore, is not an accident but a necessity. Instead of civilization being artificial, it is a part of nature, all of a piece with the development of the embryo or the unfolding of a flower.

'There is warrant for the belief', Spencer later rejoiced, 'that Evolution can end only in the establishment of the greatest perfection and the most complete happiness.' Similarly, Brace completed thirteen readings of *The Origin of Species* with the comforting assurance that evolution guaranteed the final triumph of human virtue and the perfectibility of man. 'For if the Darwinian theory be true, the law of natural selection applies to all the moral history of mankind, as well as the physical. Evil must die ultimately as the weaker element in the struggle with good.' In fact, by its very nature, the doctrine of evolution appeared to hold out to its followers the prospect of an eventual millennium. In the meantime, it offered comforting intellectual and moral reassurance to the self-reliant individualist and believer in *laissez-faire*.

In addition to its other applications, the theory of evolution appeared to many to offer guidance in the political sphere. Here the concept of evolution could become the basis of an extreme individualist anticollectivist philosophy. Only the unhampered development of the individual personality in unfettered competition with others, as Spencer never wearied of stressing, permitted the operation of 'natural selection' in the social sphere and produced its full beneficial results. Even individual selfishness and greed, in conditions of competition, could be vehicles of social progress. Competition assured the 'survival of the fittest'. Outside interference with the beneficent mechanism served merely to retard the march of progress. Thus evolution in the social sphere, in the classical formulations of Spencer, provided a new philosophical basis for uncompromising economic (and indeed political) liberalism. The findings of Darwin underscored the doctrines of Adam Smith. Yet, if evolution supported liberal individualism, it had, at the same time, important conservative connotations. Just as natural selection as a scientific hypothesis reduced to a minimum the role of mutation in the evolutionary process, so evolution, as a social doctrine, implied the rejection of violent, radical or catastrophic change. Evolutionary processes, on the contrary, are by their very nature so slow as to be virtually imperceptible. In its political applications, in fact, the evolutionary hypothesis stipulated an essentially conservative-liberal or liberal-conservative approach congenial to the successful man of affairs.

The evolutionary doctrine was not adapted merely to the ideological needs of economic and political life. Almost miraculously, it provided also a model of international relations. Even Bismarck, arch-empiricist though he was and contemptuous of 'professorial' theorizing, proved not insensitive to the widespread appeal of social Darwinist concepts. Notwithstanding the partial contradiction between them, both prosperity and war, the two major features of the age, could be accommodated, thanks to evolution, within the framework of a single all-embracing world view. Indeed, evolution achieved the near-miracle of linking in a unified, mechanistic, non-theological system individual, group, nation and mankind, and activities as diverse as commerce, warfare and religion. Here was an explanatory model, resting on the elegant simplicity of a few neat and intelligible propositions. Whatever the philosophy based upon evolution may have lacked in speculative depth, it more than made up in its rationalist and almost aesthetic appeal.

Evolution, furthermore, was by definition a doctrine of movement appropriate to an age of change. The world, whether viewed as mechanism or workshop, received a new dynamic direction with everything combining to work towards an ultimate noble, if as yet imperfectly perceived goal. Not surprisingly, Darwinism, combining all these virtues, would become a major ingredient in a new secular universalist philosophy.

A variant of that philosophy, significant mainly in the light of later developments, was being evolved in Russia. There was in the Russian economic, social and political scene little warrant for a belief in self-generating progress. The improvements in conditions sought eagerly by many, especially younger educated Russians, could, it seemed, be brought about only through conscious individual effort. For this reason the seminal philosophy of Nikolai Chernyshevsky, the most influential among the new breed of radical publicists of the sixties, bears a significant family resemblance to the doctrine of Smiles. Labour and science were once again the keynotes. In fact, Chernyshevsky pinned his hopes for human betterment on the efforts of young men and women endowed with a scientific, rationalist and materialist turn of mind. His heroes (like Turgenev's Bazarov) were medical men. Their motivation – again there are echoes of Smiles – was essentially egoistic. 'Hitherto,' muses one of them, 'I have not been foolish enough to make sacrifices, and I hope that I never shall. My interest clearly understood is the motive of my acts. . . . It is in my own interest that I always act.'

Self-interest, rationally understood, embraced in Chernyshevsky's view also the service of humanity. 'You were harming the cause of mankind', one character lectures another, 'and betraying the cause of progress. That . . . is what is called in ecclesiastical language the sin against the Holy Ghost, the only unpardonable sin.' The prime object in Chernyshevsky's view must be the self-expression of the human personality. 'Come up from your caves, my friends,' he adjures his readers, 'ascend.'

Come to the surface of this earth where one is so well situated and the road is easy and attractive! Try it, development! development! Observe, think, read those who tell you of the pure enjoyment of life and of the possible goodness and happiness of man.

Read them, their books delight the heart, observe life – it is interesting; think – it is a pleasant occupation. And that is all. Sacrifices are unnecessary, privations are unnecessary, unnecessary. Desire to be happy: this desire, this desire alone is indispensable. With this end in view you will work with pleasure for your development; for there lies happiness.

Chernyshevsky's unoriginal philosophy is significant since it formed the staple intellectual diet of at least two generations of Russian radicals. Lenin, himself an admirer of Chernyshevsky's work, would one day hail him (with little enough justification) as 'a great socialist' and a precursor of Bolshevism. Abundant evidence testifies to the impact of Chernyshevsky's ethic on Russian radicals. Just as Spencer held out hopes of a 'brave new world' to American businessmen, so Chernyshevsky did to Russian radicals. The 'Great American Dream' and 'Soviet Man' share a common intellectual ancestry.

Yet, despite its wide currency, the ideology of progress did not pass unchallenged. 'Excelsior' was the 'strange device' written on the banners of its numerous anti-materialist, anti-capitalist and anti-industrialist critics. William Blake, long ago, had vowed not to rest till he had 'built Jerusalem in England's green and pleasant land'. Wordsworth in turn had conjured up the shades of John Milton in defence of 'altar, sword and pen, Fireside, the heroic wealth of hall and bower'. 'We are selfish men', had been his despairing cry. In the forties, Thomas Carlyle, the 'Sage of Ecclefechan', opened his life-long crusade against the vices of bourgeois industrialism. In *On Heroes and Hero Worship and the Heroic in History*, he had extolled the militant virtues of Mohammed, Luther, John Knox and Cromwell, the spiritual militancy of Dante, Shakespeare, Dr Johnson and Robert Burns. (Emerson almost simultaneously had included in his list of spiritual heroes Plato, Luther, Shakespeare, Montaigne, Milton, George Fox, Goethe and Napoleon.) It was a curious antithesis to Smiles's industrial worthies. Yet ironically, notwithstanding their widely contrasting ideals, Carlyle and Smiles, besides their personal friendship, shared common moral ground. It was to Carlyle that Smiles owed his conviction of the moral (indeed religious) significance of labour, his admiration for strength of character in face of adversity and for single-minded dedication to the accomplishment of worthy tasks. However diverse their choice of 'heroes', both Carlyle and Smiles admired certain 'Puritan' virtues – moral earnestness, austerity, hard work and perseverance. Indeed, the Scots Calvinism they shared could sustain both the industrial ideal and its moral rejection. Thus in *Past and Present*, in the hope of 'perhaps illustrating our own poor century thereby', Carlyle had contrasted the firm and wise rule of a medieval abbot and the nineteenth-century decline of paternalist authority. In *Oliver Cromwell's Letters and Speeches* he had commended the militant crusader and 'man of God' to the admiration of his countrymen. Throughout a long literary career Carlyle, with an enthusiastic following of younger men, continued his single-minded crusade against the philosophy of progress.

The fervour of 'our philosopher Mr Carlyle' attracted the sarcasm of, among others, Anthony Trollope. If Carlyle was right, he wrote, they were all going 'straight away to darkness and the dogs', but then he did not put much faith in Mr Carlyle, 'nor in Mr Ruskin and his other followers'. The loudness and extravagance of their lamentations, the wailing and gnashing of teeth which came from them over a

20, 21 Samuel Smiles, author of *Self-Help*, and Thomas Carlyle, historian and lifelong crusader against the vices of bourgeois industrialism.

world which was supposed to have gone 'altogether shoddy-wards', were so contrary to the convictions of men who could not but see how comfort had been increased, how wealth had been improved and education extended, that the general effect of their teaching was the opposite of what they had intended. It was regarded simply as 'Carlylism' to say that the English-speaking world was growing worse from day to day.

In France Ernest Renan put forward Carlylean arguments in a thoughtful article in the *Journal des Débats* in 1855. It was a searching critique of the International Exhibition on the Champs de Mars, the pride of official Paris. Times and countries, Renan claimed, where comfort had become the principal public attraction were the least gifted with regard to art. This was the reason for the general lack of nobility (*noblesse*) which characterized British taste in every sphere. It explained also the general desire for well-being and the bourgeois airs which English habits everywhere carried with them. Women were also to blame for demanding of their menfolk wealth and vulgar luxury rather than heroic enterprises.

The lack of grandeur and hence of poetry, Renan continued, which marked the major achievements of the century reflected an essential characteristic of modern times. Craftsmanship and industry were good, but they were not liberal arts. The merely useful could never ennoble. Industry rendered immense services to mankind but these were, after all, services paid for with money. Let everyone have his due reward, the useful man an earthly one, wealth, happiness in an

55

earthly sense, all the blessings of the earth. To the genius, virtue, glory, nobility, poverty. If the qualities which made an industrialist did not wholly preclude moral elevation, they did not necessarily presuppose it. It was wrong to attach to useful and honest things the notions of glory, splendour, poetry which in the past had been reserved for matters involving the moral and intellectual qualities of man. It was a mistake to regard wealth and utility as the measure of social rank. This was a fact little understood by people who, dazzled by the great industrial advances of the times, imagined that such progress signalled a revolution of the human spirit. Such people mistook the accessories of civilization for its essence. 'Do not let us be surprised therefore,' Renan wrote, 'if our industrial jubilee has neither inspired nor produced anything of a spiritual order.' Were the crowds which had thronged the crystal vaults of the Exhibition more enlightened, more moral, more truly religious than their ancestors of two centuries before?

Renan's attack drew a characteristic rejoinder from the pen of Adolphe Guéroult, a publicist and politician of Saint-Simonian leanings. Did not Renan, Guéroult asked, feel some scruples about denigrating achievements to which he owed not merely the roof that gave him shelter, the clothing that protected him and the food that sustained him, but also the thousand and one refinements so many ingenious minds had exerted themselves to produce to make life pleasant, agreeable and easy? Furthermore, if people were now able to devote themselves to the search for the true and to love of the good, was this not because industry was freeing them from the yoke of material circumstances?

Industry was harnessing the forces of physical nature and setting them to work for the benefit of man. The misery or at any rate the straitened circumstances of the great majority of mankind still impeded the moral and intellectual advancement of humanity. If people desired the greatest possible development of the forces of industry, it was because they saw in chemistry, in engineering, in credit, the indispensable tools of humanity. Until these forces had assured even the least of men sufficient leisure, mankind would remain enslaved to the drudgery of material labour. Thus Renan, Guéroult argued, was wrong to consider the arts superior to industry. True, something was still lacking before industry would rise to the heights of its new destiny. This was the consciousness of its social and religious nobility.

22, 23 Justus von Liebig, the chemist for whom British civilization rested on coal, and John Ruskin, stern critic of industrialism.

Industry was like a *parvenu* who had made his way by himself and had not yet found time to reflect on his role and mission. It had not yet been guided or inspired by anything higher than selfish love of gain.

The first of Guéroult's themes, his appeal to love of comfort, was rejected with scorn by the intellectual critics of prosperity, and his concluding argument perhaps carried greater conviction in 1855 than it would twenty years later. Nevertheless, his central point at least, his belief in the progressive liberation of mankind from material drudgery, was telling. What use, indeed, were the ideals of the intellectuals to the masses often lacking in education, leisure and even minimal respite from manual labour and fatigue? On the other hand, had Guéroult really answered Renan's charge that the 'ideals' of industry were ignoble, mean and selfish, anti-cultural, anti-spiritual, anti-poetic and anti-aesthetic?

The argument assumed a variety of forms. Matthew Arnold, for instance, took issue with John Bright, for him the very embodiment of complacent philistinism, for praising the thoughtfulness and intelligence of North Americans as a nation of newspaper-readers with an interest in politics. Arnold sided with Renan, who had charged them with a 'want of general intelligence', or culture. His conclusion was that 'in the things of the mind, and in culture and totality, America, instead of surpassing us all, falls short'. Ruskin, on the other hand, another critic of industrialism, chose as his victim the unfortunate chemist Justus von Liebig. The latter had described civilization as 'the economy of power' and identified coal as the source of Britain's

57

power. This, for Ruskin, was 'the maximum of folly of modern thought in this respect'. 'Not altogether so, my chemical friend,' he protested. 'Civilization is the making of civil persons, which is a kind of distillation of which alembics are incapable and does not at all imply the turning of a small company of gentlemen into a large company of ironmongers.' As for British power (what little was left of it) being coal, that was by no means the case.

Another representative critic of industrialism and the ideology of progress, the Swiss historian Jacob Burckhardt, commiserated with a friend on the pervasiveness of coal. In London, he wrote, the stuff had given him a permanent feeling of nausea 'not so much on account of its messiness as because of its being the true symbol of all the repulsive modern life-rush'. Coal was modernity in all its obnoxious persistence. Much reading of Greek texts had induced in him 'a true scorn for our century and its pretensions'. The great misfortune of the age dated from the previous century, particularly from Rousseau's theory of the goodness of human nature. Ordinary people and the educated classes alike had distilled from this the doctrine of a golden age that must inevitably follow if only noble human nature were allowed free rein. The result, as every child knew, was the complete dissolution of the concept of authority. In the minds of the intelligent classes, the idea of natural goodness had turned into that of progress – that is, uninhibited money-making and comfort, with consciences salved by philanthropy. There was only one possible cure, that at long last this insane optimism should once more disappear. Contemporary Christianity was inadequate, since for a century it had been entangled with the prevailing optimism. Change would and must come – but only after immense suffering.

Burckhardt's pessimism was shared by, among others, Richard Wagner, who in *Rheingold* (1869) and *Die Walküre* (1870) used medieval German myth as a vehicle of protest against the materialist spirit of the age. Siegfried, noble embodiment of heroic Germanism, was confronted by mean monsters and greedy dwarfs which, without much difficulty, could be identified as representatives of capitalist attitudes. In a similar vein the young Nietzsche, shortly after the defeat of the Paris Commune in 1871, rejoiced that not everything had yet been ruined in the midst of 'Franco-Jewish shallowness' and the greedy milling around of the present. Bravery still existed – German bravery. As early as 1855 the novelist Gustav Freytag in *Soll und*

Haben, a novel which won wide popularity, especially among young middle-class readers, had contrasted 'honest' German business methods and 'crooked' Jewish ones. In the late sixties, the attack on plutocracy (not infrequently with anti-Jewish overtones) gathered pace, to reach a crescendo after the collapse of prosperity in 1873.

The preoccupation with biology expressed, among others, in Darwin's *Origin of Species* (followed in 1865–66 by the Austrian monk Gregor Mendel's epoch-making formulation of the laws of genetic inheritance), stimulated interest in questions of race. In 1853–55 the anti-Semitic French diplomat Arthur de Gobineau had published his four-volume *Essai sur l'inégalité des races humaines*. This, at least in some circles, established his reputation as an ethnologist, and 'anti-Semitism' came to be accepted as a new 'scientific' term. A partial English translation of Gobineau's work appeared as early as 1856. While racialism was not a major ingredient in the 'anti-progressive' ideologies of the age, its emergence was not without significance for the future.

While it is possible to question the practical influence of ideology in general, that of the 'anti-progressive' ideologies of the age of optimism appears particularly problematic. In *Culture and Anarchy* (1869), Matthew Arnold's pessimistic analysis of British culture (it may be doubted whether the situation differed materially elsewhere in Europe), the 'Barbarians' of the ruling class are depicted as, on the whole, devoid of intellectual curiosity or interests. The 'Philistines' of the middle classes lacked 'sweetness and light' while the 'Populace', with very occasional exceptions, existed below the level of the 'higher culture' altogether. But who listened to the lamentations of a handful of intellectuals and aesthetes about the absence of 'the noble' and 'the heroic' in the life-style of the age, about its lack of taste, its preference for an English philosophy of comfort, its growing industries symbolized by the hated coal? Though dissident intellectuals were appointed to university chairs (mainly of history and philosophy) in increasing numbers, especially from the late sixties onwards, there is poignancy in Burckhardt's lament in 1872 that young intellectuals who only a decade before would have sought academic, clerical or bureaucratic careers had transferred their allegiance to 'the party of business'. It was, beyond a doubt, the positivist ideology which enjoyed the larger following.

IV THE CULTURE OF
PROSPERITY AND ITS CRITICS

The culture of the age of prosperity, reflecting the general world view and tastes of the rising bourgeoisie, could be seen, at any rate in one of its aspects, as essentially a culture of *nouveaux riches*. The most glittering – indeed the exemplary – *parvenu* society, derided as such by critical contemporaries, was to be found not in England but in the Paris of Napoleon III. This was the society which – with the Empress Eugénie the arbiter of fashion – set the tone for the rest of Europe. The first cultural manifestation of the Second Empire – its culture has been aptly described as a form of bourgeois Rococo – was the setting provided for the International Exhibition of 1855. At the 'highest' cultural level, this included traditional elements. Ingres, Delacroix and Decamps dominated the associated exhibition of contemporary European art. Serious musical offerings included Meyerbeer's *Etoile du Nord*, the 'success of the year', as well as several works by Verdi (who had reluctantly composed *Les Vêpres Siciliennes* in honour of the occasion). Berlioz's *Te Deum* received its first performance. But more characteristic of the cultural tastes of many Parisians were Offenbach's *Bouffes Parisiens*, opened in the summer of 1855. Equally, it was the lighter side of Parisian entertainment which proved the major attraction for visitors to the Exhibition.

Among these visitors, for the first time, were to be found middle-class British tourists in considerable numbers. It was for them that Thomas Cook provided the first excursions to the Continent. His clients, it was noted, differed in significant respects from the traditional aristocratic travellers. Unlike their predecessors, they travelled mainly by rail, considered by the snob a sign of vulgarity. 'Going by railway', growled John Ruskin, 'I do not consider as travelling at all; it is merely being "sent" to a place, and very little different from becoming a parcel.' Unlike their predecessors also, travellers like the clients of Thomas Cook did not, as a rule, speak French. It was at the time of the Exhibition of 1855 that the words 'English spoken here' began to appear in French shop-windows.

61

24 Offenbach's *opéra bouffe* typifies the cultural extravaganza of the Second Empire.

A significant stimulus to British middle-class travel was not the only by-product of the Paris Exhibition. If that Exhibition helped to establish the idea of 'gay Paree' in a number of British homes, it also set off the Second Empire on its glittering course of cultural extravaganza. While provincial France, under the influence of Catholic morality, maintained anti-cultural attitudes of 'puritan' narrowness, sophisticated Parisian culture was characterized by wit, irreverence and frivolity – with an occasional admixture of maudlin sentimentality. Parisians thronged the *Bouffes* to applaud the repertoire of Offenbach and his brilliant librettist Halévi, patronized the *comédies de mœurs* of Augier, Dumas *fils* and Victorien Sardou, and revelled in the sentimental emotionalism of Gounod's *Faust*. Operetta, virtually a new art form, achieved an unprecedented popularity. *S'amuser*, to be entertained, was the object of the hour. The result, all too often, was vulgar frivolity. When, in 1867, Napoleon and Haussmann unveiled the new Opéra to the public gaze, '. . . it was like a wedding cake . . . it glittered in white and gold.' Visitors to the Exhibition that year commented on the lack of taste in French clothes, furniture and pottery. The brothers Goncourt were scandalized at spotting among the exhibits funeral wreaths wrought in porcelain.

Fashion, meanwhile, was dictated by the *nouveaux riches* who had invaded the *salons* of the capital. Bright colours were the *dernier cri* (magenta was invented at the time of the battle, in 1859), as was brightly dyed auburn hair. The *grande dame*, copying the style of the *demi-monde*, considered it *chic* to act the part of the *lorette*. Galop and *cancan* were the rage. Some female dress assumed a masculine appearance, with society beauties sporting tail-coats, collar and tie, Zouave jackets and officers' waists, canes and monocles. On the other hand Charles Frederick Worth, the English dressmaker destined to rise to fame and fortune dressing fashionable Paris society, including the ladies of the imperial Court (the House of Worth dates from the year 1858), designed the crinoline in 1855 to conceal the interesting state of the Empress Eugénie. Copied at once by Queen Victoria, it remained for years the fashion on both sides of the Channel. Its popularity provoked the satire of Daumier who was led to speculate, pictorially, on its possible usefulness as a parachute. If, in fact, the style of the Second Empire had some of the aspects of a bourgeois Rococo, it sadly lacked the grace and charm of the original. Eugénie de Montijo, notwithstanding her undoubted talents as a leader of fashion, bore as

25 Queen Victoria and Prince Albert received by the Emperor Napoleon and the Empress Eugénie at the Hôtel de Ville, Paris in 1855. The newly designed crinoline heightens the glitter of the occasion.

little resemblance to the elegant, graceful and empty-headed daughter of Maria Theresa (to whom, however, she had vowed something of a cult) as did Offenbach's Belle Hélène to Mozart's Donna Elvira. Critics of Parisian society were not wholly wrong in castigating its frivolity, shallowness and lack of taste.

Artists, on the other hand, the quality of whose work transcended the Parisian frivolities, often had to contend not only with the self-appointed guardians of Neoclassical or Romantic purity but with a censorious official prudery (not uninfluenced by the régime's need to conciliate Roman Catholic opinion). Thus, while the jury in the art

63

exhibition of 1855 happily hung acres of Ingres and Delacroix, it rejected the entries of the 'contemporary' (Realist) Courbet. Flaubert, following the publication of *Madame Bovary* (1856–57), was accused of having 'under the pretext of painting character led the way to a realism which would be the negation of the good and the beautiful'. Prosecuted for the alleged immorality of the novel, he narrowly escaped conviction. Baudelaire, some months later, was less fortunate. For producing *Les Fleurs du Mal* he was (together with the printers and publishers) sentenced to a fine. Six of the poems were banned. In 1861, it was the turn of Richard Wagner, a performance of whose *Tannhäuser* provoked a riot. Four years later, journalists and public professed to be scandalized by the unconventionality of Manet's *Olympia*. 'A deliberate manifestation of inconceivable vulgarity,' 'this Olympia, a kind of female gorilla', 'this yellow-bellied odalisk', 'art which has sunk to such a low level doesn't deserve to be condemned', were some of the critical comments. An exhibition of fifty pictures by Manet in connection with the International Exhibition of 1867, however, passed almost unnoticed. A public brought up on the canons of academic classicism and historicizing Romanticism on the one hand, on *esprit*, cynicism and sentimentality on the other, did not take kindly to works of the *avant-garde*, whether Realist or Neo-romantic.

Nor were the wider preoccupations of the age conducive to the refinement of public taste. A complete civilization, Renan vainly admonished, must take account of art and beauty as much as of moral and intellectual development. Times and countries where comfort had become the principal public attraction had been the least gifted in the arts. Baudelaire in his turn warned against 'the modern idea of progress applied to the fine arts'. It was, in his view, 'a grotesque idea', an 'infatuation symptomatic of a decadence already all too visible'. The eyes of 'zoocratic and industrial philosophies' must be opened to the 'differences which characterize phenomena of the physical and the moral world, of the natural and the supernatural'. Painting was 'an evocation, a magical operation', art a profound moral imperative, necessary to any society worthy of the name.

Artistic sensibility, however, was not to be commanded. In vain did Baudelaire appeal to the middle classes: 'You are the majority both in numbers and intelligence, so you have the power and can dispense justice.' They were well-to-do and well informed. It was their duty,

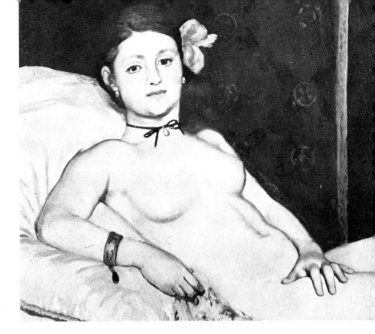

26 Manet's *Olympia* (detail, *right*) shocked official and critical opinion.

therefore, to enlighten others, to welcome beauty, to feel it. Art was 'an infinitely precious possession', not to be scattered or squandered. For a nation to drop behind in art and politics was nothing less than suicide. But Baudelaire's pleas availed no more than the sharp shafts of Daumier who, in the pages of *Le Charivari*, flayed the incurable philistinism of the French bourgeoisie.

In England, similarly, critics bewailed the state of culture in an increasingly industrial society. Matthew Arnold, among others, deplored the lack of refinement of the 'Philistines'. It was with them that the future of British culture rested, and he ardently prayed that their vigour and moral earnestness might be softened somewhat by a touch of 'sweetness and light'. William Morris, in his turn, complained that the only care of the middle-class public was for excessive opulence and that they conceived of art as 'going hand in hand with luxury'. There was, in the public of the day, no real knowledge of art and little love for it. All that survived was at best 'certain vague prepossessions', the mere phantom of that tradition which once bound artist and public together. Neither a pastoral nor an agricultural people, John Ruskin pontificated, could produce art while it remained at peace. Commerce was not, perhaps, inconsistent with art but could not produce it. Manufacture not only was unable to produce it but invariably destroyed whatever seeds of it existed. In fact, no great art

65

was possible for a nation save that which was based on battle. No great art ever rose on earth except among a nation of soldiers.

In the eyes of intellectuals, industrial preoccupations were fatal not only to the arts but to cultural interests in general. Ferdinand Lassalle, for instance, the intellectual leader of German socialism, in 1864 castigated the cultural sterility of the contemporary German bourgeoisie:

> To think of this general descent on the part of the middle class in the land of Lessing and Kant, Schiller, Goethe, Fichte, Schelling and Hegel! Did these intellectual heroes merely sweep above our heads like a flight of cranes? What is the curse that has disinherited the middle classes so that . . . no single drop of refreshing dew has ever fallen upon their steadily decaying brains? They celebrate the festivals of our great thinkers because they have never read their works. If they had read them, they would burn them.

Looking at the situation from a somewhat different angle, a German publicist noted in 1858 that a nation of 'forty million dreamers and idealists' had learnt a good deal in the hard school of reality:

> Romanticism and sentimentality, transcendental philosophy and supra-nationalism, have now withdrawn from the public life of our people into private life. For realism and steam, machines and industrial exhibitions, the natural sciences and practical interests now fill the great market-place and work at the humming loom of our time.

No less detrimental to the progress of German culture was the emergence of a new and strident nationalism. Whereas during the fifties representative public monuments still commemorated 'poets and thinkers' (Herder 1850, Lessing 1853, Schiller, Goethe and Wieland 1857), none was erected in the sixties. Instead, from 1864 onwards, Germany became engrossed in the task of national unification, commemorated in the end (1873) by the hideous Victory Column (*Siegessäule*), landmark of the new imperial Berlin. Its British equivalent, the scarcely less hideous Albert Memorial, attempted, at any rate by comparison, to commemorate cultural achievements. The Prince Consort, in fact, held in his hands the catalogue of the Great Exhibition of 1851. Later, moreover, his monument would be flanked by the Royal Albert Hall.

27–29 Germany honours culture: memorial to Goethe and Schiller (*left*) raised in Weimar in 1857. Sixteen years later, Germany glorifies her might: the Victory Column in Berlin, erected in 1873 (*centre*). London's Albert Memorial (*right*) at least commemorates the arts of peace.

Nor did the much-increased wealth of the German *haute bourgeoisie* in the late sixties and early seventies promote the cause of culture. To the super-patriotism and 'Sedan smile' reflected in a mass of popular patriotic poetry was now added the vulgar ostentation of *nouveaux riches*. These were busy constructing their pretentious town residences on the Kurfürstendamm in Berlin with heavy neo-classical façades, vast internal parade staircases, ornate mirrors and chandeliers, and palatial reception- and dining-rooms. Artistic pretension, as a rule, stopped at the vast flower-pieces painted by the fashionable Makart, or the ornate decorative scenes of Piloty. All was done with the single object of impressing. In a similar spirit the (basically modest) Alfred Krupp designed for himself the massive pile of the Villa Hügel, completed in 1873. Only the Court in Munich remained something of a cultural oasis, under the eccentric Ludwig II, patron of Wagner and builder not only of the Festival Hall in Bayreuth but of the vast neo-Gothic castles of Hohenschwangau and Neuschwanstein.

Nor was the cultural impoverishment of the period confined to Germany. On the contrary, it was (with the doubtful exception of pre-industrial Russia) a general European phenomenon. This was demonstrated in connection with the greatest technical achievement of the age, the cutting of the Suez Canal. Although 245 books, articles and pamphlets were published about the Canal in 1869–70, Europe's intellectuals failed to produce a single worthy memorial. Distinguished correspondents – W.H. Russell, H.M. Stanley, G.A. Henty, Zola and Gautier – attended the opening, but they wrote no books. Ibsen contrasted the imposing engineering feat of the Canal with the narrowness of Norwegian life, but gave the mighty Nile preference over both. Verdi, after twice refusing the commission to compose an opera, finally completed *Aïda* almost a year after the official opening. Significantly, it was left to science and tourism – represented respectively by seven Egyptologists and by Thomas Cook – to profit from the occasion.

Yet, despite generally unfavourable conditions, the age of prosperity attempted in certain directions to develop a style of its own. At one moment it bade fair to become an 'iron age', not only in its railways (the 'iron way' in every major European language except English) and its diplomacy of 'blood and iron' but also in its building. As early as 1850, Théophile Gautier had argued that it was necessary to

create a totally new architecture, born of today, now that use is being made of new systems created by the industry that is just coming into existence. The application of cast-iron allows and demands the use of many new forms, such as can be seen in railway stations, in suspension bridges, in the arches of greenhouses.

Within a year, thanks to Joseph Paxton, erstwhile head gardener to the Duke of Devonshire turned architect, Gautier's dream became reality. The first sketch, significantly, of the design for the Crystal Palace was drawn by Paxton on a piece of blotting-paper at a board-meeting of the Midland Railway (of which he was one of the directors). It was iron which, in the completed building, formed 'the weblike structure of thirty-three hundred columns and twenty-three hundred girders' that supported nearly a million square feet of glass. 'Take iron and glass,' *Punch* represented Prince Albert as saying, 'and, beauty wedding strength, produce the Industrial Hall of Nations.'

Here indeed was an architecture seemingly attuned to the new industrial age. Paxton combined in his person and career so many facets of the age that Briggs has not hesitated to call him 'the "complete

30 The studio of Hans Makart, whose vast and ornate flowerpieces delighted the *nouveaux riches* of Berlin.

man" of Victorian England'. Of his building a critic wrote, 'We have been saved from a hideous and costly mass of brick and mortar, and have a graceful and beautiful creation in its stead, . . . a new and suggestive *fact*, a step taken along a fresh track. . . . Architecture had to wait for help from a botanist.'

While not everyone agreed with this panegyric – Disraeli for instance sarcastically referred to the Crystal Palace as 'that enchanted pile' – many believed it to be the architectural pattern for the future. Gilbert Scott, probably the most successful British architect of the period, expressed the view that 'this triumph of modern metallic construction opens out a new field for architectural development' (a field, however, which he himself scarcely chose to enter). In fact, some of Paxton's most enthusiastic disciples were to be found in France. 'Iron, iron, nothing but iron!' Haussmann admonished the architect commissioned to design the new Paris central market. Baltard demurred. 'He was an obstinate type and a hardened classicist,' Haussmann later recorded.

Iron! It was all right for engineers, but what did an architect, an
artist, have to do with this industrial metal? What? He, Baltard, a
Grand Prix de Rome, who made a point of never introducing into
his projects the smallest detail that was not justified by proper
precedent, compromise himself with a building material which
neither Brunelleschi nor Michelangelo nor any of the masters had
used! . . .

Les Halles duly rose in the style pioneered by Paxton. So did the
Palace of Industry, built for the Exhibition of 1855, almost a replica
of the Crystal Palace itself. Iron was used in important structures on
both sides of the Channel, among them the interiors of the University
Museum in Oxford (1855) and the Bibliothèque Nationale in Paris
(1868), as well as several office buildings. Even a church (St Eugène)
was constructed with iron piers and iron rib-vaulting. Yet, though
iron was clearly the 'contemporary' medium, it never quite succeeded
in establishing itself. Whether in response to the dictates of public
taste (or that of individual patrons) or in pursuance of their own
inclinations, leading architects and art theorists, Pugin, Gilbert Scott

31, 32 'Iron, iron, nothing but iron!' said Haussmann, and in this new Iron Age of Europe bricks and mortar gave way to cast iron in some important buildings. (*Opposite*) Upper gallery of the Crystal Palace (1853); (*right*) Oxford University Museum (1855).

(the designer of St Pancras Station in London) and Ruskin in England, Viollet-le-Duc in France, the architects of Cologne Cathedral in Germany, in theory and practice championed the neo-Gothic style. It was this which, by and large, prevailed in representative public buildings (English 'railway Gothic', Cologne Cathedral, the fortifications of Carcassonne, the new town halls of Vienna and Munich). Paxton himself, the architect of the Crystal Palace, accepted a commission to design the Rothschild castle of Ferrières. Iron remained in the main the construction material of industry (bridges, iron-framed factories) and civil engineers. It would achieve its apotheosis in 1889 in the shape of the Eiffel Tower.

'Il faut être de son temps' was the motto also of Edouard Manet, painter of boats and railways, of open-air concerts and ('scandalous') picnic parties, of barmaids, tipplers and soldiers. Realism, it has been claimed, was 'the hallmark of the mid-century decades', the counterpart to the development of science and technology, to the Crystal Palace and the *Origin of Species*. Prominent among its pioneers was Gustave Courbet, a socialist who proudly (if not quite logically) proclaimed himself as 'without ideals and without religion'. Of his picture

71

Stonebreakers (1850) he wrote: 'I have invented nothing. I saw the wretched people in this picture every day as I went on my walks.'

A huge canvas, *Burial at Ornans*, exhibited with *Stonebreakers* at the Salon of 1850, established Courbet as the acknowledged leader of the Realist movement. For the International Exhibition of 1855, he prepared a large allegorical painting, *M. Courbet's Studio*. In the centre, Courbet showed himself, working at a canvas with a landscape and watched by a farmer's boy and a nude model (with her clothes scattered provocatively around her). On the left he depicted other models, including a gravedigger, a prostitute, a Jew, a huntsman and an Irishwoman in rags. On the right appeared Baudelaire (the leading protagonist of Realism among the critics) and Proudhon (whose full portrait Courbet had painted two years earlier). Among the many couples peopling the scene, one represented Fashionable Love, the other Free Love. When the jury rejected *M. Courbet's Studio* (as well as *Burial at Ornans*), Courbet exhibited them with others of his paintings in a separate pavilion called 'Realism', which he set up close to the main Exhibition Hall.

Prominent among Courbet's *sujets* were realistic nudes, one of which caused the late-Romantic Delacroix to comment that 'the vulgarity and pointlessness of the conception' were abominable. By 1860, however, Courbet, without ceasing to be both a Realist and a Socialist, was mellowing. His painting lost its rigid, doctrinaire character. Sainte-Beuve was led to speculate (1862) that it was Courbet's idea 'to look on vast railway stations as new churches for painting and to cover the big walls with a thousand subjects ... picturesque, moral, industrial ... in other words, the saints and miracles of modern society.' Nothing, in fact, was further from Courbet's mind. Rather than becoming the artist of industry, he now painted, realistically, landscapes and seascapes, sensuous nudes and flower-pieces. By the mid-sixties, official opposition to his work had ceased. He had become a regular exhibitor at the Salon (though, in 1871, he would find himself in trouble after having been pressed into service by the Commune).

Other Realist painters of the period included, besides Manet, the *paysagiste* Corot, in Baudelaire's view 'at the head of the modern school', Millet, the sentimental 'poet' of rural labour, Gavarni with his lithographs of Parisian life, and the great caricaturist and satirist Honoré Daumier. In England, a conspicuous representative of Realism

33 *The Stonebreakers* by Gustave Courbet, pioneer of the Realist movement. 'I have invented nothing. I saw the wretched people in this picture every day as I went on my walks.'

was William Frith, painter of large crowded canvases (*Ramsgate Sands* 1854, bought by Queen Victoria, *Derby Day* 1858, *Paddington Station* 1862, and *The Marriage of the Prince of Wales* 1865, painted for Queen Victoria), who acquired a European reputation.

Another facet of Realism was reflected in the meticulous concern with accurate detail in historical paintings like the vast battle scenes of Horace Vernet, who was patronized by Napoleon III, or Meissonnier, Adolf Menzel's scenes from the life and times of Frederick the Great, or Anton von Werner's pictorial representation of the Proclamation of the German Empire at Versailles. Even painters associated with the Pre-Raphaelite Brotherhood, a belated (non-Realist) offshoot of German Romanticism, succumbed to Realist theory. Truth, which was their goal, according to Ford Madox Brown demanded that the painter of a historical picture should make himself thoroughly familiar with the character of the times and the habits of the people he meant to depict. He must consult the proper authorities 'for the costume . . . architecture, vegetation or landscape, or accessories'.

34 *M. Courbet's Studio*, detail.

35 (*opposite*) The rejection by the 1855 exhibition jury of Courbet's entries provoked the satire of Daumier: 'This M. Courbet . . . nobody is really as ugly as that!'

Holman Hunt in obedience to the same philosophy, in 1854 went to
the length of visiting Palestine so that the Dead Sea in *The Scapegoat*
should be correctly drawn. Madox Brown, in his programmatic
picture *Work*, included not only a realistic representation of Hamp-
stead but clearly recognizable portraits of Carlyle and the Christian
Socialist F. D. Maurice. Pre-Raphaelitism in fact, from the first, had
been something of a literary ideal.

In literary theory also, Realism was in the ascendant. The American

Nathaniel Hawthorne, for instance, in 1860, characterized the work of Trollope as 'solid and substantial, written on the strength of beef and through the inspiration of ale, and just as real as if some giant had hewn a great lump out of the earth and put it under a glass case with all its inhabitants going about their daily business, and not suspecting their being made a show of'. Trollope's books were 'just as English as beef-steak'. Trollope commented complacently in his autobiography that Hawthorne had described 'with wonderful accuracy' the purpose he had ever had in view in his writing. It had always been his desire to 'hew out some lump of earth', and to make men and women walk upon it 'just as they do walk here among us – with not more of excellence nor with exaggerated baseness', so that his readers might recognize human beings like themselves and not feel themselves to be carried away among gods or demons.

Curiously similar to Trollope's was the approach of Russia's leading critic, Nikolai Chernyshevsky. The first demand to be made of art, he proclaimed, was 'to so represent objects that the reader may conceive them as they really are'. If the artist, for instance, wished to represent a house, he must see to it that the reader would conceive it as a house and not as a hovel or a palace. If he wished to represent an ordinary man, he must see to it that the reader would not conceive him as a dwarf nor as a giant. His own purpose in his novel *What Is To Be Done?* had been to represent 'ordinarily upright people of the

new generation' such as he had met by the hundred. He had tried to show 'human beings acting just as all ordinary men of their type act'. Such men did not act in real life differently from the way he had pictured them as acting.

Realism was fast establishing itself as the dominant trend in post-Romantic literature. Major novelists of the age – Turgenev, Flaubert, George Eliot, Tolstoy, Trollope – placed a new emphasis on the 'here and now', on careful depictions of character, social setting and physical background, often based on personal observation. 'It will be a novel of contemporary life,' wrote Dostoyevsky in 1865, characteristically, of *Crime and Punishment*, 'and the action takes place this year.' Flaubert, though he spoke somewhat ironically of 'les prétensions scientifiques qu'on a maintenant' in reference to *Madame Bovary*, deliberately set out to offer his readers a 'scientific' analysis of personality. 'I am called a psychologist,' Dostoyevsky wrote in his diary. 'This is not true. I am merely a realist in the higher meaning of the term, that is, I depict all the depth of the human soul.'

The extreme to which Realism could be carried in the historical novel was revealed in Viktor von Scheffel's carefully researched *Ekkehard* (1859). Realism of a different kind infused the dramatic poems which established the literary reputation of Henrik Ibsen (*Brand* 1866, *Peer Gynt* 1867). The major literary works of the period increasingly devoted their attention to the representation (sometimes critical) of bourgeois society (Flaubert specifically referred to *Madame Bovary* as 'un sujet bourgeois'). Tolstoy and Turgenev, however, being aristocrats, form something of an exception.

However, just as the Gothic Revival shared the stage with the Crystal Palace and its progeny, and Pre-Raphaelite Romanticism flourished side by side with the art of William Frith, so in the sphere of literature Romantic and neo-Romantic strains co-existed with the dominant realism. Poetry in particular, perhaps because of its very nature, was concerned with language, form and sound, expressed a philosophy of 'art for art's sake', and sought for a reality beyond reality. In France, the tradition, begun by Gautier, of 'l'Art pour l'Art' continued in the poetry of the late-Romantic Victor Hugo (whose work prefigures the Parnassiens, the Symbolists and the Decadents) and the movement of the Parnassiens, through Baudelaire (*Les Fleurs du Mal* 1857) to Verlaine and Rimbaud (*Le Bâteau ivre* 1871).

In England, a similar non-Realist literary strain was represented by

FitzGerald's translation of *The Rubaiyat of Omar Khayyam* (1859) and by the poetry of Dante Gabriel Rossetti. In Germany the pre-Realist tradition was transmitted through the late-Romantic Hebbel to the neo-Romantic Wagner. In short, the literature of the period, like its architecture and its painting, showed conflicting trends. Only a few major figures – Tolstoy, Turgenev, possibly Ibsen – achieved an effective synthesis of Romantic and Realist elements.

However, if there emerged some degree of equipoise in Europe's cultural élite (significantly, both the realist Courbet and the Pre-Raphaelite Millais were absorbed into their respective artistic establishments), there is no doubt about the tastes of a wider (and growing) middle-class reading public. Their preoccupations were mainly practical, at times utilitarian, directed towards concrete knowledge, popular science and technology, exploration, the description of unusual occurrences (in 1865 Edward Whymper finally succeeded in climbing the Matterhorn) and outlandish places. This orientation was clearly reflected in an *Open Letter* addressed by Thackeray to friends and readers on assuming the editorship of the *Cornhill Magazine* in 1859. The journal, he promised, would offer its readers 'as much reality as possible':

> discussion and narrative of events interesting to the public, personal adventures and observations, familiar reports of scientific discoveries, descriptions of Social Institutions – *quicquid agunt homines* – a Great Eastern, a battle in China, a Race Course, a popular Preacher – there is hardly any subject that we don't want to hear about, from lettered and instructed men who are competent to speak on it.

That this or something like it was the recipe for success is proved by *Die Gartenlaube*, a periodical started in 1853 by an ex-radical German journalist, Ernst Keil, to cater for and develop the cultural tastes of a middle- and lower-middle-class readership. Its object was to provide unpretentious family reading, for the entertainment and instruction of all its readers, irrespective of age or sex. Popular science figured prominently among the contents, and the regular contributors included the popular naturalist Alfred Brehm, whose classic *Illustriertes Tierleben* was published in 1869. Extensively illustrated (and cheaply, thanks to new processes just coming into use), it was careful to respect the prejudices of its readers. The success of the venture exceeded the wildest expectations: its initial printing of 5,000–6,000 copies had risen to 160,000 by 1863, and ten years later reached a peak of 460,000. (Even in 1885 only five out of some 2,500 German papers had a circulation above 40,000.)

Moreover, *Die Gartenlaube* was soon only the most successful of a number of similar publications: *Ueber Land und Meer*, founded in 1858, sold 55,000 copies in 1867 and 160,000 in 1872. It was family journals such as these which created in Germany, for the first time, a middle-class mass readership.

In France, at this time, the most successful venture in popular journalism was *Le Petit Journal*, a paper without any literary or artistic pretensions which reported local occurrences, gossip and scandal. Its circulation, 38,000 in 1863, rose to 270,000 in 1866 and to 300,000 in 1869–70. By comparison, *Le Figaro*, the most widely read literary and political 'quality' paper, sold 3,000 copies in 1860–61, 55,000 in 1866, and 65,000 in 1869–70.

More generally, many readers, besides seeking to be entertained, were now looking for information on practical matters. The editor of a new edition of the *Encyclopaedia Britannica* published in 1861 referred in his Preface not only to the advancement of knowledge which had made it necessary but also to 'the increased demand for works of this class by the diffusion of education throughout the country'. Equally characteristic of the practical bent of the age was the appearance in 1862 of Mrs Beaton's classic, *Household Management*; the nation which knew how to dine, the author proclaimed proudly, had learnt 'the leading lesson of progress'. In France, too, there was a widespread cult of *le practical man*, centred particularly round the personality of Benjamin Franklin. It was in this area rather than in the arts that the intellectual curiosity of the (culturally) newly enfranchised middle classes found its principal expression. In vain did Arnold, Burckhardt and Baudelaire, Renan, Ruskin, Morris and Nietzsche bewail such 'philistinism'. The emergence of a popular middle-class culture announced the approaching isolation of an increasingly esoteric cultural élite. Murger's *Scènes de la Vie de Bohème* (1845–49) inevitably appealed to a wider public than Baudelaire's *Fleurs du Mal*, and Smiles's *Self-Help* or Trollope's chronicles of Barsetshire exercised a wider appeal than *The Rubaiyat of Omar Khayyam*. The result was a cultural dualism which it would be hard to describe as equipoise. The culture of the rising middle classes must differ of necessity from that of the intellectual élite.

36, 37 The unpretentious semi-realism of *Die Gartenlaube* (*below*), careful of the tastes and prejudices of its middle-class family readership, contrasts with the heavy formalism of Fantin-Latour's presentation of the French cultural establishment in *Hommage à Delacroix* (1864). The group includes Whistler and Manet (left and right of the portrait) and Baudelaire (seated, far right).

38 Manchester, centre of British Liberalism, here symbolized by the heavy solidity of Waterhouse's neo-Gothic Town Hall.

Representatives of the bourgeoisie, similarly, made their own distinctive contribution to the politics of the age of prosperity. Liberalism
was widely considered by contemporaries the most influential
political ideology of the period. In the words of a perceptive German
publicist, it played 'a dominant role in the life of European peoples
and states'.

A broad statement of the liberal creed – romanticized, but not
therefore untypical – was that of the German historian Gervinus.
'Individualism,' wrote Gervinus in the introduction to his *History of
the Nineteenth Century* (1854), 'the self-awareness of the personality,
has become so powerful in men that it will modify political concepts
and institutions; it will dissolve the closed corporations, the states
within the state; it will eliminate all caste and class differences. The
striving for the equality of all relations, for the freedom of man
toward man, is necessarily involved in this self-awareness of the
personality.'

The nineteenth century for Gervinus was, *par excellence*, the century
of liberation. 'The emancipation of all the oppressed and suffering,'
he wrote, 'such is the call of the century. The might of these ideas has
triumphed over powerful interests and deep-rooted conditions, in the
abolition of servile dues and obligations in Europe and the emancipation of slaves in the West Indies. This is the great movement of our
time.' Gervinus's pronouncement was a classic statement of the
universalist liberationist version of the liberal creed. In the words of a
historian of British liberalism, 'emancipation from traditional bond-
ages and restraints found its political expression in being a rank and
file liberal'.

Such a view of liberal universalism, however, clashed with a very
different, quasi-Marxist interpretation, propounded by, among
others, a well-known German radical of 1848 turned moderate.
Liberalism, asserted Julius Froebel, was by no means to be understood
as implying popular freedom in general. Rather, it was 'a system in
the interest of quite specific elements of society which are assembled

in the commercial and industrial middle-class'. The liberal state in the conventional sense was the state which represented the interests of this social group. It did not necessarily represent the interest of other classes of the population or even the interest of the majority. It was round the two poles represented respectively by Gervinus and Froebel that the discussion of liberal ideology revolved.

Gervinus's broadly based liberal philosophy was, particularly during the sixties, widely diffused among intellectuals and in ruling circles in several parts of Europe. A striking illustration of its impact is provided by the far from enthusiastic emancipation of the Jews in the Grand Duchy of Baden. There the Grand Duke, in 1862, had addressed himself to his Minister, Lamey, to learn his views on the subject. Lamey, referring to debates in the Second Chamber two years earlier, replied that people in the last decade had 'lost the courage' to oppose Jewish emancipation on grounds of principle. Instead, they had argued that it was, for the moment, inopportune. In opposition to this view, Lamey argued that the constitutional structure of the Grand Duchy 'no longer allowed' the exclusion of a class of subjects from a number of civic functions simply because of their religion. Piecemeal concessions were no longer possible, only total emancipation. No doubt it was still necessary to overcome a certain repugnance in accepting Jews on a footing of equality. There was, for Germans, something about them that was alien and uncongenial. On the other hand, Jews were citizens. If they were considered to be Germans and Badeners, one must draw the logical consequences. In short, general liberal attitudes had become so strong that it was no longer possible for a reluctant Minister to delay Jewish emancipation.

By contrast with this and a number of similar instances of the impact of Gervinus's 'liberalism of emancipation', Froebel's 'liberalism of the commercial and industrial classes' was represented above all by the philosophy of the 'Manchester School' – a term accepted throughout Europe as a synonym for economic liberalism. Typical of this aspect of liberalism was John Bright's argument that 'all legislative interference with the labour market, all attempts of Government to fix the wages of industry, all interference of a party between employers and employed are unjustifiable in principle and mischievous in their results', or Herbert Spencer's view that trade unions were harmful because they interfered with the freedom of working-men to dispose of their labour.

Nowhere was the liberal ambivalence between broad humanitarian principles and hard-nosed economic and political interests revealed more clearly than in the field of primary education. Here, while there is no doubt of the zeal and sincerity of campaigners like Cobden or Smiles, it is equally certain that other liberals welcomed elementary education mainly as a weapon against 'intemperance, pauperism and perhaps trade-unionism'. Political considerations often outweighed social concern over the problem of illiteracy. Mevissen, a liberal German industrialist, deplored that the rule of the masses had begun in Europe, though they had not been trained to rule, and considered that they 'must still acquire the measure of self-control necessary for the achievement of social purposes'.

In England, Robert Lowe echoed Mevissen. Commenting on the Reform Act of 1867, of which he disapproved, he declared that the extension of the franchise made it essential 'to compel our future masters to learn their letters'. When Forster introduced the second reading of his Education Bill in the House of Commons, he argued that 'the good, the safe working of our constitutional system', as well as the future of British industrial and military strength, depended upon the speedy provision of elementary education. Questions had to be answered and problems solved which ignorant constituents were ill-fitted to solve.

Arguments such as these were a far cry from Gervinus's concern with the emancipation of the human personality and the 'freedom of man toward man'. In fact, the often ambivalent character of liberal attitudes and policies reflects to a certain extent the social composition of liberal parties or movements, more especially that of their parliamentary leadership. The composite nature of that leadership was analysed in a perceptive article in a conservative Prussian journal. Its author examined the membership of lower chambers in France and Italy, as well as in Germany and Prussia, and sought to determine the nature of 'that new bourgeoisie which stands apart from the masses'. He succeeded in identifying three distinct strands. The first and most important consisted of men who had acquired a higher education by attending a secondary school and a university, but had remained 'virtually strangers to the actual realities of life, in other words, men of abstract education which instructs about everything and nothing'. In this category, the writer placed judicial officials, administrative officials, to a considerable extent the clergy, physicians, scholars, teachers at the higher levels, lawyers and similar people. In a second group he placed those who had acquired a modern education but whose intellect had been trained at the expense of their spiritual sensitivity: the engineers, higher technicians, men of letters, 'especially Reformed Jews, and others of that sort'. Finally, there were the bigger merchants, manufacturers, artificers, managers, 'noble landowners who have given up the old traditions [i.e. who had adopted capitalist techniques and attitudes] and others of that sort'. Not all the members of these occupations belonged to the new bourgeoisie, but it was from their ranks that it was chiefly recruited. Such, the writer concluded, were the enemies of legitimate government, i.e. the liberals.

This Prussian conservative prudently confined his analysis of liberals to those of continental Europe. British liberalism, reflecting at the same time a more advanced industrial society and a unique aristocratic social system, had distinctive characteristics which differentiated it from its continental counterparts. Almost alone, it could attain executive power by constitutional means. If landowners, lawyers and businessmen have been seen as 'the three great castes' within the British Liberal party, superficially, at least, it was the first who predominated. Of 456 Liberal M.P.s representing English constituencies between 1859 and 1874, half were either large land-owners or their sons; 198 had an annual rent-roll exceeding £2,000.

On the Liberal front bench, on the other hand, it was men with a commercial background or with substantial business interests (though not infrequently they were landowners at the same time) who formed the majority. Gladstone, though a landowner who had married into the landed gentry, not only came from a family of wealthy Liverpool merchants but was also a considerable coal-owner. Like Cardwell, another landowner and offspring of a wealthy Liverpool merchant family, he retained his Liverpool business connections. Childers and Goschen, 'the plutocratic element', were closely connected with the City of London. Childers, for instance, in the intervals of his political career, became chairman of an English bank and an Indian railway, deputy chairman of an Australian bank and a director of several English railways. Bright and Forster were northern industrialists. Granville, the obligatory peer (as Foreign Secretary) in Gladstone's first administration, was an ironmaster and the largest employer of labour in Hanley. Hartington was heir to a property at least as much industrial as it was agricultural. Lowe, with (exceptionally) a professional background, was regarded by his colleagues as a spokesman for *The Times*, for which he wrote until 1867.

Of Liberal back-benchers, roughly a third had active commercial or industrial interests. One-fifth had received a legal education and practised for at least a number of years. Those with commercial interests included well-established businessmen like Gurney, Grenfell and Glyn. There was a Rothschild, and three or four representatives of the China firm of Jardine, Matheson & Co. The cutting-edge of the parliamentary party, however, was provided by 'about thirty or forty great capitalists, Dissenters almost to a man'. These included men like the radical activist Samuel Morley, a wealthy hosiery-manufacturer from Nottingham; William Rathbone, a Liverpool merchant prince, 'astute machine politician' and founder of the District Nursing Movement; Doulton, the china-manufacturer; and Crosland, a woollen-manufacturer from Huddersfield. Crossley's carpet factory in Halifax, in one generation, had become, with 6,000 employees, the largest in the world, while the numbers employed by Platt, manufacturer of textile machinery in Oldham, rose from 2,500 in 1854 to 7,000 in 1872.

Northern industrialists such as these have been aptly described as 'the world of Samuel Smiles in its second generation, the fortunes having been made, but social assimilation by polite society having still to do its deadly work'. Others, the Gladstones and Cardwells, the Goschens, Childers and Rothschilds, were already assimilated both socially and politically into the world of aristocratic parliamentary politics. The middle class in business, it has been said, 'was entering politics by absorption, not by conquest'. They were 'doing it through the mines, banks, railways, the City and shipping interest, that dominant part of the business world with which committees of the Commons were so entangled and in which the best blood of the land had long co-operated with complete equanimity'.

Were men like Delane of *The Times* and Trollope justified in complaining that the aristocracy was being swamped by a flood-tide of plutocracy? It appears that nothing could be further from the truth. Not only were industrial and commercial men, even in the parliamentary Liberal party, deeply embedded in an aristocratic-landowning milieu and an aristocratic tradition of government. The strength of the aristocratic system, both socially and politically, was such that it could comfortably absorb the newcomers.

85

So vast is their traditional power [wrote a contemporary observer in 1867], so broadly does it sit over the land, so deep and ancient are its roots, so multiplied and ramified everywhere are its tendrils and creepers and feelers that the danger is never lest they should have too little, but always lest they should have too much power, and so, even if involuntarily, check down the possibilities of new life from below.

The reasons for the continued influence of the aristocracy were, besides the wealth (landed, urban and industrial) of many of its members, the social homogeneity and cohesion of the estate and the deference readily paid to its members by the rest of the population.

They have a common freemasonry of blood [noted an observer], a common education, common pursuits, common ideas, a common dialect, a common religion and – what more than any other thing binds men together – a common prestige, a prestige growled at occasionally, but on the whole conceded, and even, it must be owned, secretly liked by the country at large. All these elements, obvious in themselves, but difficult to measure and gauge, go to make up that truly and without exaggeration tremendous consent of power, often latent, often disguised, which constitutes the indirect representation of the aristocracy in the House of Commons.

In vain did Cobden think of pitting the middle classes against this influence when he wrote (1862) that, for all their faults and short-comings,

our mercantile and manufacturing classes as represented in the chambers of commerce are after all the only power in the state possessed of wealth and political influence sufficient in part to counteract in some degree the feudal governing class of the country.

John Bright could rhapsodize about cotton as 'the magic impulse which has been felt . . . in every department of national energy, which has affected more or less our literature, our laws, our social condition, our political institutions, making almost a new people.' In fact, the total number of liberal Lancashire mill-owners has been estimated, from trade directories, as not greatly exceeding 500. As Gladstone pointed out, throughout the industrial and commercial community there existed 'a sneaking kindness for a Lord'.

39 Richard Cobden and John Bright, twin champions of Manchester commercial and industrial interests.

The reality, subtler than Cobden or Bright perceived, was not confrontation but a social compromise, assimilation and amalgamation, of which Gladstone himself was a striking example. In his compromise the top strata of the bourgeoisie, intermingling with the landed aristocracy, abandoned their once self-consciously aggressive stance. John Bright himself mellowed perceptibly in his later years under the influence of social acceptance by the Russells and the young Whigs, the Cavendishes, Amberleys, and Trevelyans. Moreover, this occurred at the very time when the aristocracy itself was experiencing a decline both in corporate self-consciousness and in its will to govern.

It was the coincidence of the two trends that made possible the 'Gladstonian compromise'. That compromise, ardently propagated by Matthew Arnold, among others, was facilitated by the public schools. Their contribution to the amalgamation of aristocrat and commoner should not be underestimated. Cheltenham, Marlborough, Radley and Rossall had functioned since the forties, Wellington since

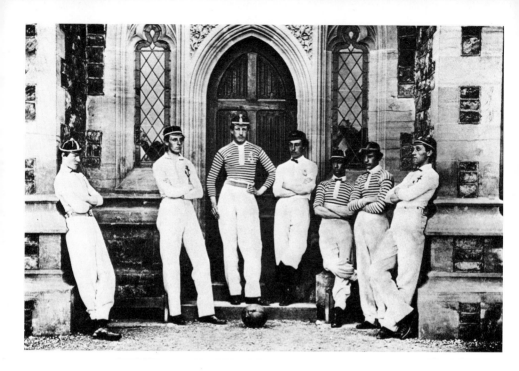

1853. Clifton, Haileybury and Malvern dated from 1862. Schools such as these provided for future administrators and politicians a common ethos of hard work and plain living, of games, classics and chapel, irrespective of descent from landed baronet, banker or prosperous professional man. The products of this educational process, moreover, were coming in increasing numbers to occupy leading positions in politics, the civil service, business and the professions. The hereditary landed aristocracy and an almost equally hereditary aristocracy of wealth were being steadily welded into a new ruling élite.

In France, the social groups which in Britain furnished the bourgeois element in the parliamentary Liberal party were divided in their political allegiance. On the one hand, important commercial, industrial and banking interests, representing the ruling financial-political oligarchy of the July Monarchy (including the Paris Rothschilds and the establishment of the Banque de France) with Thiers as their leading parliamentary spokesman, upheld in opposition to the imperial régime a cautious liberal-conservatism linked closely to the defence of property rights. Eugène Schneider, Vice-President of the Corps législatif, was not only a leading industrialist but also a Regent

40 These seven young gentlemen, 'capped' for Clifton in 1865, are typical of the future administrators and politicians nurtured by England's public schools.

41 (*right*) Henri de Rochefort, aristocratic anti-Bonapartist. His satirical journals reflected the rise of a new medium – a political Press.

of the Banque de France (as well as a friend of the Emperor). Another Vice-President, Alfred Leroux, was also an industrialist. Baroche, President of the Conseil d'Etat (1853–63) and eventually enjoying ministerial rank (1861–69), was an influential spokesman for these interests inside the imperial government itself.

As against this 'Orleanist' and, to some extent, Parisian political connection of the *haute bourgeoisie*, Republicans, led by provincial lawyers like Ollivier, Favre, Gambetta and Jules Ferry, showed radical democratic leanings. Their aristocratic ally Henri de Rochefort, with his successful satirical journals (*La Lanterne* 1868–69, circulation above 100,000; *La Marseillaise* 1869–70, 50,000–140,000), would be a thorn in the flesh of the declining imperial régime. Both groups, united in their opposition to Napoleonic authoritarianism, subscribed to certain liberal tenets and (though the term 'liberal' rarely appears in the French political vocabulary) could be regarded as separate wings of a broadly liberal movement.

The success of Rochefort's campaign against the imperial government reflected the rise of a new political medium, a Press designed to cater for a mass readership outside the ranks of the traditional cultural and political élites. This, ranking among the most significant developments of the age, was to be observed in every major country. It was Great Britain, however, which led the way. Here, the impact of the Crimean war and the accompanying craving for news produced a significant increase in newspaper sales: the daily circulation of *The Times* rose between 1853 and the summer of 1855 by 14,000 copies, that of the *Illustrated London News, News of the World* and *Reynolds Weekly* by 50,000, 45,000 and 20,000 a week respectively. The turning-point, however, in the development of the British Press came with the repeal of the stamp duties in June 1855. This made possible London's first penny paper, the *Daily Telegraph*, which, by 1870, sold 170,000–190,000 copies (as against *The Times*'s 70,000). Moreover, spurred on by the success of the *Telegraph*, the *Standard* and the *Daily News* became penny papers respectively in 1858 and 1868. It was, however, the family papers which enjoyed the largest circulations (*Reynolds Weekly* in 1861 sold 350,000 copies) followed by the popular dailies (the *Telegraph* selling 150,000 copies in 1861, the *Standard* 130,000).

Meanwhile, the total number of papers in the United Kingdom rose from 795 in 1856 to 1,450 in 1871. Particularly striking was the growth of the provincial Press. Of a total of 546 million copies sold during 1864, 340 million were of provincial publications. The *Manchester Guardian*, previously a bi-weekly, became a daily in 1855, as did the Edinburgh *Scotsman*. This rapid expansion of the British Press also made the fortune of Julius Reuter, who had opened a modest news agency in London at the time of the Great Exhibition.

Much of the growing Press, predictably, was liberal in its political sympathies. Of the London dailies, for instance, it has been said that 'the *Telegraph* served the Liberalism of convention, the *Daily News* the Liberalism of conviction'. Both regarded themselves and their readers as identified with the fortunes of the Liberal party. In Lancashire, more than forty liberal journals outnumbered twenty conservative ones. The radical *Manchester Daily Examiner and Times* within the space of five years increased its readership from 18,000 in 1856 to nearly 40,000. The *Daily News* was part-owned by Samuel Morley, who enabled it not only to become a daily but also to buy up a smaller radical paper. In return, he influenced the paper's political attitude, threatening more than once 'in the event of a line of opposition to Mr Gladstone being persisted in', to 'discontinue his connection with the paper'.

42 The Hoe ten-feeder press, bought from America by *The Times* in 1857.

Similar developments of the Press occurred in other countries. New publications included the *New York Times* (1851), the business journal that would gain fame as *Die Frankfurter Zeitung* (1856), *Le Temps* (1861), and the *Neue Freie Presse* of Vienna (1864). In 1866 *Le Figaro*, a weekly since 1854, became a daily.

As in Great Britain, much of this Press was liberal in its political complexion. *Le Figaro* and *Le Siècle*, both moderately liberal, at the end of the decade had a combined circulation of 100,000 as against a mere 8,500 for the imperialist *Le Constitutionnel*. Mass-circulation papers, moreover, promoted the diffusion of liberal attitudes among the middle classes. The *New York Tribune* for instance, founded in 1841 by the erratic liberal Whig Horace Greeley, was strongly abolitionist in its sympathies; in 1860 it was selling 200,000 copies a week. In Germany, the mass-circulation *Die Gartenlaube* (p. 77), though not primarily political in purpose, adopted, at least down to 1866, a liberal stance in deference to the presumed preferences of its readership. Papers such as these made a significant contribution to the spread of liberal ideas.

Notwithstanding, however, the support of much of the new Press, the political path of liberalism was far from smooth. Everywhere conservative influences barred the way. In countries such as Prussia, Austria and France, monarchical officials, largely exempt from parliamentary control, blocked progress. So, in Great Britain, Austria and Prussia, did traditional landowning and aristocratic interests, strongly entrenched in conservative second chambers. Strong groups of artisans, notably in parts of Germany, resented the advance of capitalism and its concomitant, bourgeois liberalism. There was hostility also among members of intellectual establishments, committed either to romantic conservatism or to a socialist philosophy.

91

43 Pope Pius IX, offered the cap of Liberty by Garibaldi in this cartoon as 'more comfortable' than the papal tiara. His answer was the *Syllabus Errorum* and the dogma of papal infallibility.

Not least, the Churches, in an age of reviving religious interest, turned increasingly against both liberal ideology and liberal policies. Relations between Church and State, above all control of education, became in many countries important political issues.

On the European continent, the opposition to liberalism on these and other issues was led by the Roman Curia. In the aftermath of the revolutions of 1848 Pope Pius IX had taken up his life-long fight against liberal infiltration of the Catholic Church. His aim was the extension of clerical influence and the formulation of an integral doctrine of anti-liberalism as the basis of Catholic orthodoxy. Monarchies weakened by revolution were willing to co-operate, particularly in Catholic countries, seeking by appropriate concessions to secure the support of the Curia internationally and that of the hierarchy, the parish priests and those whose political consciences they directed, in internal politics. In France, the Loi Falloux of 1850, sanctioned by the Prince-President for political reasons, gave private persons – which in practice meant Roman Catholic organizations – the right to open secondary schools. Within a year, more than 250 new educational establishments were founded, mainly by religious orders.

In 1850, also, the territorial Catholic hierarchy, suppressed at the Reformation, was re-introduced in Great Britain in the face of fierce opposition. The crowning political achievement of the papal counter-revolution, however, was the Concordat signed in 1855 with the

Austrian government. Described as 'the farthest point reached by the Austrian government in its march back from 1848', this placed the Church under the special protection of the State, gave bishops complete control of Catholic education and restored ecclesiastical courts.

Parallel with his political successes, Pius IX assumed the offensive also on the ideological front. In December 1854 he proclaimed – significantly without the concurrence of a General Council – the dogma of the Immaculate Conception of the most blessed Virgin Mary. Driven increasingly on the defensive politically by the Italian *Risorgimento*, from the later fifties he redoubled his efforts to forge an anti-liberal ideology, at the same time asserting his own spiritual autocracy. A lengthy preparatory process (initiated as early as 1854) resulted in the promulgation late in 1864 of the *Syllabus Errorum*, accompanied by the Encyclical *Quanta Cura*. In a covering letter Cardinal Antonelli, the Papal Secretary of State, informed bishops (many of whom must have known better) that never since the beginning of his pontificate had Pius IX 'ceased to proscribe and condemn the chief errors and false doctrines of our most unhappy age'. Among these the Syllabus listed the view that the Roman Pontiff 'can, and ought to, reconcile himself and come to terms with progress, liberalism and modern civilization'.

The final crown of the papal edifice was the proclamation at the Vatican Council of 1870 of the doctrine of Papal Infallibility in matters of religious dogma. The doctrine, rejected by German 'Old Catholics', became the occasion of a severe political conflict in the new German Empire when the Curia demanded that the German governments should dismiss 'Old Catholic' teachers. In the ensuing *Kulturkampf*, German liberals and the new German state stood ranged against the Papacy and the great majority of German Catholics in a struggle over the twin issues of Church control over education and State control over German Catholicism. The 'May Laws' passed by the Prussian Landtag in the spring of 1873 ushered in an open trial of strength. It would reveal the political power of German Catholicism.

In Great Britain, the confrontation of Church and State assumed somewhat different forms. As in the Catholic Church, strong anti-liberal elements were at work in the Church of England. 'My battle,' Newman later wrote of the Oxford Movement, 'was with liberalism; by liberalism I meant the anti-dogmatic principle and its developments . . . such was the fundamental principle of the Movement of

93

1833.' In political terms, the Church of England was defending the freedom of its voluntary schools from State control, the levying of compulsory Church rates, the maintenance of discrimination against Dissenters and the continued ascendancy of the Anglican Church of Ireland. Against this Dissenters, with the exception of Methodists, rallied to the Liberal cause and called not only for equal rights but for the disestablishment of the Church of England as well as of its Irish counterpart. The Liberal party, Anglican in its leadership but dependent for political effectiveness largely on the nonconformist vote, had to steer a careful course between liberal principles and the claims of dissenting supporters on the one side, the needs of social stability and the 'Gladstonian compromise' on the other.

In the face of various obstacles, particularly in the political sphere, the progress of liberalism in the fifties was relatively slow. After the failures of 1848 its prospects, with reaction in the ascendant, at first looked bleak. A break in the reactionary front, however, occurred in 1855 with the accession of Alexander II to the Russian throne. Three years later the newly installed Prussian Regent inaugurated the political course of cautious (and largely verbal) liberalism known as the 'New Era'. After the creation, under the auspices of Cavour, of an Italian monarchy based largely on liberal principles of government, the liberal trickle became a flood. In 1861, the Russian serfs were liberated. In 1860 and 1861, Napoleon III took the first tentative steps towards the liberalization of the imperial régime in France. Elections held in 1861 and 1862 to the Prussian Landtag returned liberal majorities. The year 1865 saw the triumph of the abolitionist North in the American Civil War.

Although there were setbacks (Bismarck's appointment to the Prussian premiership in 1862, the partial purge of liberals from the Russian administration after Karakozov's attempt on the Emperor in 1866), Europe in general entered the economic and political crisis of 1866–67 with the tide of liberalism running strong. Liberalism emerged strengthened. The Reform Act of 1867, a milestone in British political evolution, was followed in 1868 by a Liberal election victory and the formation of the first unambiguously Liberal administration. In the Habsburg monarchy, the *Ausgleich* of 1867 was accompanied by the installation of a mainly bourgeois ministry of liberal complexion. In Prussia and the North German Confederation liberals, in the guise of National Liberals, became Bismarck's majority

44 Tsar Alexander II, who in 1861 decreed the liberation of the serfs – a significant
step in increasing freedom in Europe.

party, while in France, developments were set in motion that would
culminate in the proclamation of *l'Empire libéral* and a Ministry headed
by Emile Ollivier. Indeed, by 1870, liberals appeared well set towards
gaining a preponderant political influence in many parts of Europe.
Yet only in Britain did they effectively control the executive and
enjoy, within the limits of the politically feasible, a broad legislative
initiative.

Indeed liberalism, as a European political movement, was labouring
under important handicaps. In the first place – notwithstanding
isolated exceptions like the sale of monastic lands in southern Italy –
it had, on the whole, little to offer to peasant voters. Being, in many
countries, a movement directed by bourgeois 'notables', its relations
with the working class were often ambivalent. As early as the sixties,
in fact, liberals were threatened with competition from socialist
groupings such as Lassalle's organization, and the SPD in Germany.

45 William Ewart Gladstone, whose first administration (1868–74) marked the apogee of British Liberalism in this period.

Finally, there was something of a gap between articulate liberal 'notables' and the often apolitical society around them. Nowhere did liberalism enjoy an effective popular base except in Great Britain – with its distinctive alliance with nonconformism – and France, where there was localized working-class support for republicanism. Liberalism, almost everywhere, remained suspended between largely inarticulate (often 'pre-political') masses, and monarchists, aristocrats and bureaucrats whom it had little hope of controlling. Except possibly in Great Britain, the social and political basis of liberalism was precarious.

Yet in spite of the obstacles they faced, and though their interest in social as distinct from political issues was often limited, liberals left their imprint on important areas of legislation. Nowhere was this more conspicuously the case than in Germany, where a new nation – though neither a new society nor a new political structure – was being created in part under liberal auspices. Bismarck discussed many of his legislative proposals with the liberal leader Bennigsen. These included not only uniform legal procedures, a uniform coinage and a uniform system of administration, but also measures embodying more specifically liberal principles, such as the removal of restrictions on freedom of enterprise and of movement and the constitutional guarantee of freedom of the Press. Of special significance was the law of 1873 which exempted German cities from the authority of the usually conservative Landräte. This would become the starting-point for a remarkable and distinctive development of municipal institutions.

Achievements of a similar character, if on a lesser scale, stood to the credit of Thiers, Gambetta and Favre, the fathers of the Third Republic in France. In Britain, Gladstone's first administration made its contribution towards political modernization through measures like the Ballot Act, the abolition of the purchase system in the army, the opening of the civil service to competition, removal of disabilities from Dissenters and the attempt to remove some Irish grievances. The rights of trade unions and of women also received a degree of modest recognition. Though the scope of much liberal legislation was limited, the statement that liberalism 'was satisfied by sound government in the aristocratic tradition' does less than justice to its positive achievements.

Nor should the liberal contribution in the educational field be underestimated. In France Victor Duruy, Minister of Education from 1863 to 1869, did much with liberal and anti-clerical support to undo the effects of the Loi Falloux. During his term of office Duruy not only developed education at all levels but considerably strengthened the secular principle. His most controversial proposal, to make primary education free and compulsory, was vetoed in the end by the Emperor and, shortly thereafter, Duruy lost his post. In Britain, on the other hand, liberal concern with education was documented in Forster's Education Act which, though a compromise with the 'voluntary' principle of denominational education, laid the foundation of a system of State schools.

Though not in its essence a legislative or regulative philosophy, liberalism had a significant influence on the political physiognomy of the age. At any rate in the industrial countries liberal politicians created if not the social at least the political conditions in which the bourgeoisie could pursue its activities with a minimum of interference and develop its talents and civilization. Among the factors facilitating some liberal objectives, frustrating others was the widespread warfare of the period and, with it, the increased importance of military affairs.

46 Prussian officers on horseback.

47 'Here, and there': the German satirical journal *Kladderadatsch* shows Bismarck painting Napoleon as a fiend – and vice versa. The object of the two artists was to make their respective taxpayers more ready to foot the bill.

*Hey!
David
Enjoy the
(essay)
Amy)*

Military preparations and wars were, as at all times, in the first place the responsibility of governments. Governments of the period were ready, in varying degrees, to go to war for the attainment of objectives ranging from territorial aggrandisement (sometimes in the guise of national unification) to the pursuit of national interests (real or imagined), the quest for influence and the search for enhanced prestige of rulers or ruling groups. Among reasons for a widespread willingness of governments to consider war as a possible continuation – in the words of Clausewitz – of diplomacy by other means, was a relative absence in several countries of financial constraints such as had existed during the preceding decades.

Even though Austrian and, at times, French finances were in a less than flourishing state – Austria for instance had to forego, for financial reasons, a much-needed re-equipment of her armed forces in the early sixties – most countries in general could, in an age of economic expansion, assume substantial peacetime military burdens. Misgivings about the cost of military programmes such as were expressed, for instance, in Prussia before 1861 were, as a rule, confounded by buoyant revenues. Equally, the cost of short wars at any rate could be borne by most major countries without serious ill-effects. The Prussian government, to its joy and amazement, found itself able to finance the entire Danish war of 1864 from revenue and reserves. Wars, in fact, though frequent, were short. The wars of 1854 and 1859 were brought to a halt by Napoleon III, the first because it had become unpopular in France, the second on account of the threat of Prussian intervention combined with Catholic misgivings. Those of 1864, 1866 and, to some extent, that of 1870, were terminated relatively speedily by the military superiority of one of the parties, combined with some threat of outside intervention.

Other considerations also made war relatively acceptable to governments. With the exception of the *Risorgimento* and the French war *à outrance* after the collapse of the Empire (both resented accordingly by 'legitimate' governments) wars were non-revolutionary, largely non-ideological and, indeed, 'respectable'. Control remained firmly in the hands of legitimate governments which both made war and concluded peace, usually with scant regard for public opinion. Perhaps for the first time a violent outburst of public opinion in Paris in July 1870 – product of growing literacy and the democratization of politics – may partly have forced the hand of government.

As a rule, moreover, the fate of a régime was not at stake even in the event of defeat. The fate of Napoleon III, taken prisoner on the field of battle, was exceptional, as were events in the French capital after the defeat of Sedan. Peace settlements (with the doubtful exception of the Treaty of Paris) were moderate until Versailles in 1871, and did not cripple the vanquished, though, inevitably, thoughts of revenge persisted for greater or lesser periods, as in Austria after 1866. Moreover, at the beginning of a conflict, the contestants as a rule appeared more or less evenly matched, with both sides believing in the possibility of victory. Neither in 1866 nor in 1870 was the outcome regarded anywhere in Europe as a foregone conclusion. In these circumstances, governments had no overriding reason to reject war as an instrument of policy.

Wars, in fact, occurred when at least one party desired to wage them. This was the case with Napoleon III in 1854, 1859 and, with his Ministers, in 1870. It was the same with Bismarck and Moltke in 1864, 1866 and 1870. At the same time, a number of potential wars were averted because governments wished to avert them. British involvement in the American Civil War was avoided partly through the statesmanship of the Prince Consort but mainly because of the reluctance of the Union government to add to the number of its enemies. A war against Russia over Poland in 1863 was prevented to some degree, perhaps by the deterrent effect of Crimean memories but largely by the resistance of French financial interests and British 'isolationism' and suspicion of France. Again, in 1864, the majority of the British Cabinet, mobilized by the Queen, resisted any move by the Prime Minister and the Foreign Secretary that might have involved England in the Danish war. A weakening French Empire accepted (as it was unlikely to have done in the fifties) the moral defeat of Sadowa, the Luxemburg rebuff of 1867 and the humiliating conclusion of the Mexican adventure. England, by now quasi-isolationist, resigned herself in 1870–71 to the Russian denunciation of the Treaty of Paris.

48 Napoleon III on his way to surrender after the Battle of Sedan. Unusually, this was not only a military defeat but the end of a régime.

In short, as many potential wars were averted as wars actually fought. England in particular, chastened by the Crimean fiasco, strove steadily to avoid international entanglements. Palmerstonian diplomacy had had its day before Palmerston's death in 1865.

In general, however, it remains true that war was not unacceptable to the bulk of Europeans. A further reason for this was that the impact of wars, though the number of combatants might run into six figures, still remained relatively slight. Their duration (unlike that of the American Civil War) was measured, as a rule, in months (sometimes weeks) rather than years. Only where a fortified place prolonged its resistance (Sevastopol 1854–55, Paris 1870–71 and Plevna 1877), did operations extend beyond the 'respectable' campaigning season (May or June to September). Thus, if warfare was no picnic or summer vacation, neither, despite such climatic vagaries as frost and gales in the Crimea, heat in northern Italy, rain, mud and cold in France, was

49, 50 (*Left*) 1855: French troops returning in triumph from the Crimea. (*Right*) 1871: German troops on the Place de la Concorde in Paris.

it as a rule the ordeal it would later become. At the same time, and despite the increasing use of railways, wars were remarkably limited in geographical extent, with the partial exception of that of 1870. Most were confined in the main to a single relatively limited region: the Crimea, Lombardy, Schleswig, Bohemia. The Franco-Prussian war alone formed a partial exception owing to the unprofessional prolongation of resistance by the French Government of National Defence. With wars circumscribed in both time and space, civilian populations, as a rule, suffered little more than temporary inconvenience.

Nor, at least until the Franco-Prussian war, were casualties inordinate. Some 9,000 dead were buried at Magenta, under 8,000 after Sadowa. In 1866 the cholera victims – with the disease spreading from the theatre of war – far exceeded in number the battle casualties. Total casualties at Sedan numbered 26,000, of whom fewer than 9,000 were German. As against this, the American Civil War, in this respect also the first 'modern' war, claimed more than 600,000 dead (359,000 Union soldiers, 258,000 Confederates). Total casualties at Gettysburg (over 50,000) were double those at Sedan. Yet the Franco-Prussian

war, the first 'modern' war in Europe, produced, largely thanks to the prolonged French resistance, unprecedented casualties. The French lost 156,000 killed in little more than six months' fighting, the Germans 28,000. The Seven Weeks' war, in fact, was the last of the 'mini-wars'.

Until then, however, casualties among both combatants and populations had been modest. So, to the end, was the amount of actual fighting – as distinct from often wearisome marches and exposure to inclement climate, sickness and disease – a soldier was likely to see. While Napoleon was sickened by the carnage of Solferino and even Bismarck felt qualms at the sight of the battlefield of Sadowa, the 'horrors of war', so far as the belligerent populations were concerned, remained relatively remote. The cost of war, in human terms, was one most people not directly involved could contemplate with at least some degree of equanimity. It would take a scandal like the field hospital at Scutari or the inadequate care of the wounded at Solferino to provoke a public outcry. In this lay another reason why governments, in making their decisions about war and peace, were not as a rule seriously hampered by opinion.

The public, moreover, spoke almost invariably with a divided voice. Different classes, reflecting differences of interests, education and values, tended to assume divergent attitudes towards armed conflicts in which their countries were – or might be – involved. Aristocrats and landowners, as a rule, accepted war as a necessary fact of international life. It was they who staffed the foreign ministries and embassies which conducted the game of international diplomacy in which war had a recognized place. As policy-makers, aristocrats like Palmerston, Russell, Stratford de Redcliffe, Cavour, Bismarck, Gorchakov, or the Duc de Gramont were entirely ready to involve their countries in war (Bismarck, for example, once described war as 'the natural condition of mankind'), though some aristocrats – Aberdeen and Stanley are examples – were reluctant or unwilling to do so. In the divided British Cabinet of 1864 it was, on the whole, the aristocrats who were numbered among the 'hawks'.

Except in post-revolutionary France, the aristocracy also enjoyed a near monopoly of high military command. In peacetime, therefore, they represented the professional interest of their calling in dealings with governments – often of a financial or technical nature. Their outlook was shaped largely by military traditions, whether of family or 'the service'. In Prussia in particular, nobles formed a hereditary military élite. War or preparation for war was not only the basis of their education and training but, in many cases, their very *raison d'être*. As for the younger aristocrats serving in the middle and lower echelons of the more exclusive regiments (often as volunteers for a limited period), many welcomed war as a break in the routine of training, manœuvres and the social round, not to speak of tedious garrison duties. War meant opportunities for distinction, for decorations and promotion not found on the peacetime parade ground. Adventure beckoned. There was an outlet for patriotic feelings and the assertion of manhood. War, moreover, sanctioned the right to kill more effectively than did the formalized duel. In short, and for different reasons, war for many aristocrats was a not undesirable state of things. 'War goes on famously,' an English squire wrote to his son in 1854, 'and I would have it go on – wars are serviceable, as thunderstorms are – there would be no breathing at Crewe Hall between Manchester and the Potteries, but for them.'

In stark contrast to such aristocratic attitudes, commercial and manufacturing interests were, in general, pacific in their inclinations.

Be quiet Boxer, you've had enough of fighting lately!

51 As France and Austria scrap over the Italian bone, John Bull, in this cartoon of 1859, symbolizes the policy of Cobden and Bright: peace – and free trade.

Except for a small number of armaments manufacturers or contractors – and even Alfred Krupp, the 'Cannon King', was unwarlike in disposition – there was, as a rule, little profit to be found in war. However short its duration, war restricted credit, dislocated traffic and impeded production. It produced 'panics' on the Exchanges. It spelt insecurity and the interruption of every possible peacetime pursuit. War hit agriculture, depriving it of manpower and horses. It raised the spectre of increased taxation, of currency depreciation and of every kind of fiscal iniquity.

War, in short, was the enemy of prosperity. It interrupted international trade and damaged trading connections. In particular, it disturbed international financial links. The Rothschilds, for example, far and away the leading international bankers of the age, maintained autonomous branches in Frankfurt, Paris, London, Vienna and Naples. Though working closely with national governments, the branches operated as a unit for major transactions. Nothing could be more embarrassing for them than a war such as that of 1859 which pitted France against Austria. An international empire like that of the Rothschilds could thrive only in conditions of peace. James Rothschild, patriarch of the house and the uncrowned king of European high finance, consistently opposed war. In 1863, when Napoleon,

105

after much heart-searching, gave up his plans to intervene in Poland, Disraeli at any rate was of the opinion that the peace of the world, on this occasion, had been preserved 'not by statesmen but by capitalists'.

Nor was it financiers alone who tried to exert an influence for peace. Cobden and Bright, Lancashire mill-owners, between 1846 and 1851 rallied a substantial body of British opinion behind a 'peace policy'. 'Cheapness, and not the cannon and the sword,' Cobden proclaimed, 'is the weapon through which alone we possess and can hope to defend our commerce.' Free trade would 'draw men together to thrust aside the antagonism of race, and creed and language, and unite us in the bonds of eternal peace'. The desire for 'large and mighty empires, for gigantic armies and great navies, for those materials that are used for the destruction of life, and the desolation of the rewards of labour' would die away.

When in 1854 the 'Palmerstonians' prevailed over the 'Manchester men', Cobden and Bright continued their campaign in the face of almost universal opprobrium. 'Even if I were alone,' Bright exclaimed in the House of Commons,

> if mine were a solitary voice, raised amid the din of arms and the clamours of a venal press, I should have . . . the priceless consolation that no word of mine has tended to promote the squandering of my country's treasure or the spilling of a single drop of my country's blood.

Though Palmerston's star remained in the ascendant throughout the fifties, in 1860 Cobden had the satisfaction, at a time of Anglo-French tension, of negotiating the 'free trade' treaty with France which bears his name. By the mid-sixties, moreover, the pacific influence of commercial interests had succeeded in converting an important section of British opinion, not only among Liberals, to the views of Cobden and Bright. In 1864, the 'peace party' in the Cabinet, with the support of the Queen, repeatedly carried the day against 'those two dreadful old men', Palmerston and Russell.

Two years later, at a moment of European crisis, Stanley, an avowed non-interventionist, was Foreign Secretary. Anthony Rothschild, in conversation with a Saxon diplomat, summed up the pacific effect of economic interests:

The sooner we get rid of all our colonies, the better for England.

52 Although war was widely acceptable, attempts were made to limit it. Seen here is the signing of the Geneva Convention in 1864, establishing the Red Cross and defining some rules of the game of war.

We want peace at any price. It is the desire of all our statesmen. Take, for instance, Lord Derby. He owes his income of £120,000 to the fact that his estates in Ireland and Lancashire are being covered with factories and factory towns. Is he likely to support a militarist policy? They are all in the same boat. What do we care about Germany, or Austria, or Belgium? That sort of thing is out of date.

The peaceful settlement by arbitration (promoted by Gladstone) of the Alabama dispute between England and the United States marked a further success of the peace policies of the 'Manchester School'.

On the continent of Europe also, commercial and industrial interests were in general hostile to militarism. In the Prussian constitutional conflict, the liberal opposition found support from business opinion. Even after the bulk of liberals had made their peace with Bismarck, trading interests, among them the influential *Frankfurter Zeitung*, remained obstinately pacific. In France, too, the trading community was in the van of opposition to the military reforms proposed by Napoleon in 1866. Prefects from many towns reported active opposition (by the signing of petitions) from manufacturers

107

and industrialists. Military reorganization not only cost money, but also threatened to deprive rich men of the privilege of buying exemption for their sons from military service in peacetime. Such men had no wish to see their offspring spend several years in barracks in company with the sons of peasants and workers.

To the bourgeois, wrote Mérimée, the idea of risking his life had become repugnant. Those who called themselves *les honnêtes gens* considered military service 'low and vulgar'. Emile de Girardin, in his paper *La Liberté*, made himself the spokesman of the widespread pacifism of the provincial bourgeoisie. France, he argued, ought to set the example of general disarmament. 'Eaten up by the cancer of permanent armies, a veritable degenerative symptom [*dégénérescence*] of humanity', governments had the same interest as peoples in disarmament. Nor did such views fall on deaf ears. With membership of the Ligue de la Paix increasing all over France, the circulation of *La Liberté* in 1869–70 reached the respectable figure of 18,000.

If financiers and industrialists tended to begrudge military expenditure and deprecate warlike adventures, intellectuals were inclined to be militaristic and, at times, bellicose. In peace, they idealized the military virtues; in wartime they indulged in wild flights of patriotic fancy.

They justified war on a variety of grounds. Walter Bagehot, for instance, argued that the 'first work of the first ages' had been to bind men together in the strong bond of custom and that 'the incessant conflict of nations' had brought this about in the best possible way. Those primitive groups conquered which had 'the most binding and most invigorating customs'. The majority of groups which won and conquered were better than the majority of those which failed and perished 'and thus the first world grew better and was improved'. In a second stage, 'the tendency of every man to ameliorate his condition' was illogically supposed by Bagehot to have replaced war as the mechanism for securing the progress of mankind. Yet, when he formulated his 'laws or approximate laws' on 'the use of conflict', he not only laid down the blindingly obvious truth that those nations which were stronger tended to prevail over the others, but also added that the strongest tended also to be the best.

The view of militarism and war as positive moral influences was also argued on other grounds. Samuel Smiles, for instance, exalted 'the magic of drill'. Drill, he wrote, means discipline, training, education. . . . These soldiers – who are ready to march steadily against vollied fire, against bellowing cannon or to beat their heads against bristling bayonets . . . were once tailors, shoemakers, mechanics, weavers and ploughmen, with mouths gaping, shoulders stooping, feet straggling, arms and hands like great fins hanging by their sides; but now their gait is firm and martial; their figures are erect, and they march along to the sound of music, with a tread that makes the earth shake.

A few years later, during another French war scare in 1859, Smiles declared that, were the people at large compelled to pass through the discipline of the army, 'the country would be stronger, the people would be soberer, and thrift would become much more habitual'.

The views of Smiles were not unusual. While Carlyle and his admirers sang the praises of the soldier of genius, a Cromwell or Frederick II (Emerson, more impartially, included Napoleon in his Pantheon), others glorified the military virtues at a more mundane level. 'Out of fiery and uncouth material,' wrote Ruskin, only military discipline could bring forth the full force of power. Men who, under other circumstances, would have 'shrunk into lethargy and dissipation' were 'redeemed into noble life' by a service which at once summoned and directed their energies. Charles Kingsley, in one of his *Sermons for the Times*, described the transformation wrought in 'one of the worst and idlest lads' by military service. Now he 'walks erect, he speaks clearly, he looks you boldly in the face, with eyes full of intelligence and self-respect'. The true 'compulsory education', Ruskin proclaimed in 1869, was 'not catechism but drill'. It was not teaching the youth of England the shapes of letters and the tricks of numbers and then leaving them to turn their arithmetic to roguery and their literature to lust. Real education meant 'training them in the perfect exercise and kingly continence of their bodies and souls'.

Together with admiration for the military virtues of discipline, obedience, valour and self-sacrifice, went a widespread approbation of war. All healthy men, Ruskin told an audience at the Royal Military Academy in 1865, liked fighting and the sense of danger. All brave women liked to hear of their fighting and of their facing danger. This was 'a fixed instinct' in a 'fine race'. In his view, a fair fight was the best form of play and 'a tournament was a better game than a steeplechase'. The time might perhaps come, in France as well as in England, 'for universal hurdle-races and cricketing', but he did not think that 'universal cricket' would 'bring out the best qualities of the nobles of either country'.

War, in fact, was not only the foundation of all the arts ('no great art ever yet rose on earth, but among a nation of soldiers') but also of 'all the highest virtues and faculties of men'.

> The common notion that peace and the virtues of civil life flourished together, I found wholly untenable. Peace and the *vices* of civil life only flourish together. We talk of peace and learning, of peace and plenty, and of peace and civilisation; but I found that these were not the words which the Muse of History coupled together; that on her lips the words were – peace, and sensuality – peace, and selfishness – peace and death. I found, in brief, that all great nations learnt their truth of word and strength of thought in war; that they were nourished in war, and wasted by peace; trained by war and betrayed by peace.

Jacob Burckhardt, in similar vein, praised war on grounds of 'social hygiene'. After quoting, in a lecture to his Basle students in 1868, the celebrated dictum of a professor in Halle about the 'fresh and joyous war' which would 'sweep away the scrofulous scum', Burckhardt added his own approving comments. Long peace, he told the students, not only resulted in a loss of 'guts' but also produced a mass of pitiful weaklings who, without it, would never come into being. These weaklings, screaming about their 'rights', usurped the place of the 'true forces' and contaminated the blood of the nation. War would restore the 'true forces' to their rightful place and reduce the miserable weaklings to silence.

With its subordination of life and possessions to a single unifying purpose, war possessed an enormous moral superiority over the egotism of the individual. It committed individual forces to the service of a general idea and, indeed, to the highest general idea – and imposed a discipline which at the same time permitted the development of the highest virtues.

If, according to Burckhardt, war alone offered mankind the superb spectacle of universal subordination to a general idea, for others it possessed also a religious significance. 'The Lord Jesus Christ', Charles Kingsley preached, 'is not only the Prince of Peace: He is the Prince of War too.' The success of religions, claimed Bagehot, depended on their military survival value, the 'better' religions having 'a great physical advantage' over 'the worse'. Roman religion or 'the belief of Cromwell's soldiery that they were "to trust in God and keep their powder dry" were great steps in upward progress'. What Bagehot called '*fortifying*' religions – 'that is to say, those which lay the plainest stress on the manly parts of morality – upon valour, on truth and industry' – had plainly had 'the most obvious effect in strengthening the races which believed them and in making those races the winning races'.

Nor was the intellectuals' admiration for war confined to theory. When it came, they were ready to welcome it. During the war scare of 1852, Tennyson had written:

> Though niggard throats of Manchester may bawl,
> What England was, shall her true sons forget?
> We are not cotton-spinners all,
> But some love England and her honour yet.

Wellington's death, in the same year, led him to reflect that 'this nation is a great deal enervated by a long peace, by easy habits of intercourse, by peace societies and by false economies'. And when war finally came, though with Russia, not France, as the enemy, Tennyson rejoiced:

> For the peace that I deem'd no peace, is over and done,
> And now by the side of the Black and the Baltic Deep,
> And deathful-grinning mouths of the fortress, flames
> The blood-red blossom of war with heart of fire.

Kingsley meanwhile, was writing a pamphlet, *Brave Words to Brave Soldiers and Sailors*, circulated among troops in the Crimea. Recognizing that he had 'something of the wolf-vein in him', he sighed:

> Would that the Rabbits were Russians, tin-pot on head and musket in hand! Oh! for one hour's skirmishing in the Inkerman ravines and five minutes with butt and bayonet as a *bonne bouche* to finish off with!

G.J. Holyoake was a radical, but he too felt stirring within him 'an unknown and unsuspected instinct of race', leading him to wish for 'the success of England, right or wrong'. The British intellectual Establishment, in short, was filled with crusading zeal and robust patriotism. Another year's war, a radical argued, 'would show the world that there is that in Englishmen which would conquer every difficulty'. When peace was signed, Holyoake refused to illuminate his offices in Fleet Street.

The moral fervour that accompanied the Crimean war at the beginning of the period erupted once more near its end. The Franco-Prussian war, at least in England and Germany, was widely seen as an instrument of providence with German morality triumphing over French corruption. Queen Victoria set the tone when she wrote that 'it is the cause of civilisation, of liberty, of order and of unity, which triumphs over despotism, corruption, immorality and aggression'. Charles Kingsley (a Royal Chaplain since 1860) rejoiced in the German victory. 'My belief is,' he wrote, 'that it will work good for generations to come.' To a German friend, he exclaimed: 'Verily, God is just, and rules too; whatever the press may think to the contrary.' 'I am yours,' he concluded, 'full of delight and hope for Germany.' And to another acquaintance he confessed that, were he a German, he should feel it his duty to his country 'to send my last son, my last shilling, and after all my own self to the war, to get that done which must be done, done so that it will never need doing again'.

More soberly, George Eliot considered the war as one between two civilizations. With German victory, she believed, the world had entered a better phase. The Earl of Lytton, similarly, saw the Teutons as glorious and 'juvenescent' whereas France had been rotted by lies in every fibre till there remained nothing but her native ferocity. In short, for the British intellectuals, it was a victory by proxy. Seeley, Professor of Modern History at Cambridge (and successor to Kingsley, who had held the chair for nine years) summed up a widespread feeling when he wrote:

> The three principal wars of Prussia since her great disaster, those of 1813, 1866 and 1870, have a character of greatness such as no other modern wars have; the objects of them, and the spirit in which they were waged, were as high as the intelligence with which they were guided. They have in a manner reconciled the modern world to war, for they have exhibited it as a civilising agent and a kind of teacher of morals.

In fact, not a few intellectuals now looked forward with pleasurable anticipation, or at any rate without concern, to future wars to come.

Kingsley, years before, had prophesied that 'two classes . . . will have an increasing, it may be a preponderating, influence on the fate of the human race for some time . . . the man of science and the soldier.' Adolf Lasson's influential *Das Kulturideal und der Krieg* (1868) glorified the state, power and war, while Hartmann, in *Die Philosophie des Unbewussten* (1869), complacently predicted a future when, everywhere, the stronger would swallow up the weaker. Russian Panslavs (N. Danilevsky, *Russia and Europe*, and R. Fadeyev, *Opinion on the Eastern Question*, both 1869) hopefully contemplated Russia's 'inevitable' clash with 'the West' or at least with Austria-Hungary. Treitschke, on the other hand, proclaimed in the Reichstag (1871) the probable need for another Seven Years' war to safeguard Germany's recent gains. A future conflict between Germany and Russia was widely anticipated.

Nor were bellicose manifestations confined to the intellectuals. During the Crimean war, patriotic crowds roamed the streets in Birmingham, Sheffield and other cities, and a Manchester mob burnt John Bright in effigy:

> To Brighten up the Quaker's fame,
> We'll put his body to the flame,
> And shout in mighty England's name,
> 'Send him to old Nicholas!'

Bright became for many 'This broad-brimm'd hawker of holy things, whose ear is stuft with cotton, and rings Even in dreams to the chink of pence'. It was claimed that there was 'scarcely a man to be found from Land's End to John O'Groats but would like another year of war'.

Although outbursts like those in England during the Crimean war were unique (the nearest approach was the crowds parading the streets of Paris in July 1870 with cries of '*à Berlin!*'), patriotic emotions were widespread throughout Europe. In England, in 1859, 150,000 volunteers enlisted in the space of a few months to ward off a possible French attack. It was largely a middle-class movement. In France, on the other hand, during a period of much resistance to 'militarism' after 1866, the opposition among industrial workers was less violent than that of bourgeoisie and peasants. During the Prussian siege, workers rallied to the defence of Paris. Though the circumstances were unpropitious, peasants enlisted without murmur in the new armies raised by the Government of National Defence. In defence of Paris and the *territoire*, in fact, the French masses showed themselves in no way inferior in patriotism to bourgeois and intellectuals or, for that matter, to the masses in Prussia–Germany or England.

Indeed, the question may be raised why the popular masses everywhere accepted – to all appearances readily – conscript service in time of peace and active service in wartime. The available evidence does not permit a conclusive answer. Burn considers that, so far as the rural populations in England were concerned, military service may have been accepted partly as a matter of social deference. The soldier drawn from the soil would be willing to serve and fight – because his commander was the squire's son, or his equivalent. The same, *mutatis mutandis*, may well be true of the armies of Prussia and Russia. Where such 'feudal' ties had become attenuated, as in post-revolutionary France and elsewhere, other factors were likely to come into play. Both elementary and secondary education (to which at least some peasant children were gaining access) had a heavily patriotic accent, more particularly in the teaching of history and literature. So, as a rule, had military training itself, the 'university' of large numbers of young men.

The army, as William I of Prussia and von Roon clearly understood, was an instrument of solid patriotic and monarchical indoctrination, a 'school of the nation' in more senses than one. Indeed it seems likely that many a peasant passed on to his sons the lessons learnt as a conscript. It is possible also to speculate on the contribution of the clergy, whether in sermon or by precept and instruction, to the dissemination of patriotic doctrine. Priests remained influential, particularly in rural areas, throughout Europe. As for industrial workers in the towns, so many were recent migrants from the villages (with which they continued to retain contacts through family and other social ties) that their attitudes were not yet greatly different from those of the peasantry.

In any case, in a hierarchical society of 'notables', the popular masses – even where, as in France or Germany, they had the vote – remained politically inarticulate. Governments did not consult them on matters of military organizations, of foreign policy or of war and peace. These, on the contrary, were the concern of the political classes. Policy-making, essentially, was the province of small groups at the centre of power. However, with the general political advance

53 Patriotic indoctrination: *Die Gartenlaube* (1871) shows young conscript heroes returning to their native village to be crowned with wreaths by their fellow villagers.

of the middle classes, their opinions (usually expressed through the Press and sometimes the lower chambers of Parliaments) had to some extent to be taken into account. Governments could no longer afford to ignore completely – though they could still often manipulate – their views.

54 Palmerston, pointing to the map, seems to be instructing his colleagues in the Coalition ministry in the geography of *realpolitik*.

55 Cavour as Prime Minister of Italy.

VII THE NEW DIPLOMACY

The widespread readiness to accept war as a means of political decision was reflected in the international relations of the period. The age of prosperity was in fact an age also of armed conflict. The Crimean war, terminating four decades of European peace, ushered in a cycle of wars, six in number including the Russo-Turkish war of 1877. These wars, in their cumulative effect, changed the face of Europe. They destroyed the international order established by the Treaties of Vienna and recently restored after the upheavals of 1848, and replaced it by another which was very different in character.

At the same time they both reflected and promoted changes in the style of international relations. A distinctive feature of the statesmanship of the age was its relative freedom from ideological preconceptions, the blatant nature of its *realpolitik* and its readiness to resort to force in pursuit of political aims. The concept of international solidarity and the joint responsibility of governments for the preservation of peace fell increasingly into disfavour. Instead, unilateral action and the policy of the *fait accompli* became the order of the day.

The growing fragmentation of the European states' system and the absence of effective international organization which resulted, created a growing sense of insecurity, and military preparedness assumed a new importance. In fact the period from the outbreak of the Crimean war to the conclusion of the Dual Alliance in 1879 was characterized by an almost Hobbesian 'state of nature' in international relations.

It would be tempting but mistaken to link the new diplomacy with the simultaneous political progress of the European bourgeoisie and the general prosperity of the age. It would be a still greater error to associate it in any way with the systematic application of the principle of national self-determination.

Even at the height of bourgeois progress, foreign policy (except to some degree in Great Britain) was not made by representatives of commercial or industrial interests. Such men staffed neither the foreign ministries nor the embassies. Nor did they as a rule play a major part

117

56–57 These two
cartoons by Daumier
show how, in the eyes
of Europe, the Russian
Autocrat overreached
himself and plunged
into the Crimean
disaster.

in the formation of public opinion which, in any case, rarely exercised
a decisive influence.

Major policy decisions, on the contrary, were taken by a handful
of people, rulers and their immediate advisers, in Great Britain small
groups of ministers. In such circumstances even the political advance
of the *haute bourgeoisie* could have only a marginal effect. Broad
economic issues as well as matters of specific commercial interest were
subordinated, as a rule, to wider political considerations. An extreme
illustration of this is Napoleon's politically motivated support for a
'free trade' commercial treaty with Great Britain in 1860 in disregard
of the general hostility of French industrialists. Again, it was political,
not economic considerations which debarred Austria from membership of the German customs union, the Zollverein. In general, where
economic objectives clashed with political, the latter prevailed. In
1877, in a vain symbolic gesture, the Russian Minister of Finance,
Reutern, resigned his post in protest against the Tsar's decision to go
to war with Turkey.

Five practitioners of *realpolitik* – four aristocrats – Napoleon,
Palmerston, Cavour, Bismarck and Andrássy (abetted by another
aristocrat, Gorchakov), played a leading part in overthrowing the
international order set up by the Treaties of Vienna. All were opposed
– if for different reasons – to aspects of the Vienna settlement. All
acted in pursuance of limited national objectives. In pursuit of these

they brought about the piecemeal destruction of the existing international order. None of them, at least until 1879, had any new element of stability with which to replace it.

The limited ambitions which, in conjunction, produced an era of what could be fairly described as European anarchy, arose in different ways, partly out of the original Vienna settlement, partly from its restoration in 1849. They were related, also, to the political situations in the different countries concerned. Prominent among 'the five', especially in the early stages, was the Emperor Napoleon. His erratic but effective policies were inspired primarily by a desire to enhance the prestige of his shaky dynasty, as well as by a degree of sympathy for movements of nationality. The latter, however, was generally subordinated to sober calculations of French national interest. This, it was held, required neighbours who would pose no threat to France. The consolidation of Italy or Germany, therefore, must be no more than partial, with medium-sized units balancing each other and allowing France to hold the balance between them.

It was with considerations such as these in mind that Napoleon supported the extension of Piedmont 'from the Alps to the Adriatic' or of Prussia north of the Main. Moreover, whether from pure *raison d'état* or influenced by a residual concept of 'balance of power', Napoleon expected territorial 'compensations' to France for such aggrandisement as neighbours like Piedmont or Prussia might achieve. If compensation involved territories wholly or in part ethnically French in character (Nice, Savoy, French-speaking Belgium), this suited Napoleon's book but characteristically, he was quite equally ready to seek his 'compensation' in German-speaking regions on the left bank of the Rhine or in Luxemburg. In short, Napoleon's motives in seeking territorial aggrandisement were primarily dynastic and political. It was French *amour propre*, above all, that must be satisfied.

Like Napoleon, Palmerston was motivated by a mixture of *realpolitik* and ideology. It was the former which dictated the determined pursuit of British national interests, particularly in areas where sea-power could be brought to bear. These interests were held to require the continued integrity of the Ottoman Empire and Belgium. This, in turn, led Palmerston to a strategic concept of *cordons sanitaires* designed to check the presumed ambitions of both Russia and France. In this respect Palmerston could be considered a defender of the *status quo*. However, in common with British liberal opinion Palmerston sympathized – as did Napoleon – with national movements, notably in Italy and Hungary. At one with many of his countrymen, he admired Kossuth and abhorred 'General Hyena'. He also shared the general detestation of Nicholas I, particularly for his suppression of the Hungarians, but liked Napoleon with whom he held in common many political sympathies and antipathies. Being sympathetic to Italian and Magyar aspirations, he disliked the government in Vienna, while his desire for *cordons sanitaires* against potential disturbers less perhaps of the peace than of British interests, led him to view with favour (qualified, however, by concern for the Danish monarchy) Prussian ambitions in north Germany. Anti-Russian and anti-Austrian, Palmerston, if cautiously, stood emotionally and, in part, intellectually, among the 'revisionists'.

The third member of the triumvirate, Cavour, pursued relatively simple aims. It was the object of his policy to extend the sway of the House of Savoy 'from the Alps to the Adriatic' by bringing under its rule the provinces of Lombardy and Venetia. As recent events had shown, Piedmont lacked the strength to achieve her purposes unaided. Her only hope, therefore, lay in alliance with France. It was this which formed the basis of Cavour's political calculations.

It was Napoleon, Palmerston and Cavour who, in pursuit of their various objectives, presided over the first phase in the destruction of the Vienna settlement. During the second stage two new actors appeared upon the scene, in the persons of Bismarck and Andrássy. Perhaps Bismarck's major inspiration was resentment at the – to his mind humiliating – position occupied by Prussia in Germany, more particularly since the Prussian King had accepted the superiority of the Austrian Emperor at Olmütz in 1850. Bismarck desired to make the Prussian monarchy the paramount state at least of northern Germany, and Austria's equal within the Germanic Confederation. From an early moment he accepted the probability that these objectives would be achieved only by a policy of 'blood and iron'. There is no evidence to suggest that Bismarck, though ready at all times to utilize and manipulate national sentiments, was ever himself a committed German nationalist. His policy, on the whole, was opportunistic with the desire for a good understanding with Russia perhaps its only fixed point. Not until 1879 would Bismarck (after tentative beginnings in the *Dreikaiserbund*), lay the foundations of a stable European system.

Bismarck's practical aspirations went hand in hand with those of the Magyar nationalists inside the Habsburg monarchy. If Prussia had her Olmütz to avenge, they had their surrender to the Russians at Világos in 1849. They claimed the same ascendancy within the boundaries of the historic Kingdom of St Stephen, that Prussia was seeking in northern Germany. Their hope for equality with the Germans within the monarchy resembled Bismarck's aspirations for Prussia inside the Germanic Confederation. In fact, the Magyar leaders, Deák and Andrássy, were Bismarck's natural allies in his conflict with the government in Vienna.

These then were the men who, between 1854 and 1866, destroyed the Vienna system. In their foreign policy at least they were backed by national opinion (in so far as it was articulate) in their respective countries. The destruction of the Vienna system was carried out in four wars – three of them deliberately provoked. The war conducted by Napoleon and Cavour against Austria, in particular, was a totally deliberate, cold-blooded act of aggression. Linked not only by the personalities of the principal actors but also in their underlying motivation, the four wars which destroyed the Vienna order can be seen as part of a single cycle. Each of the conflicts set the stage for the next.

It is this chain-reaction which gives to the first of these wars its peculiar significance. The Crimean war (1854–56) arose out of the political circumstances of the old order, but at the same time marked the transition from the old diplomacy to the new. Like the resentments of 'the five', it arose unplanned in the aftermath of the revolutions of 1848. Those revolutions had been 'tamed' and the international order of Europe restored largely through the repeated interventions of Nicholas I. Between 1849 and 1852 when the process of restoration was completed with the London Protocol on the future of the Danish monarchy, the Tsar, pillar of the old order, appeared to be the most powerful man in Europe. But in the moment of his triumph, Nicholas I overreached himself. His attempt to 'settle' the perennial Eastern Question in Russia's favour was founded on monumental diplomatic miscalculations and conjured up an Anglo-French alliance that proved Russia's undoing.

The arrogant, opinionated and unrealistic self-assurance underlying the conduct of Nicholas I, compounded by a questionable military strategy, can be seen as the *felo de se* of the old diplomatic order. The resulting war contributed to the death of the Tsar himself, reduced

Russia's role in Europe, and embroiled her with Austria, her natural ally in the defence of the Vienna system. Indeed, following the war, Russia, smarting under the provisions of the Treaty of Paris, herself joined the ranks of the 'revisionist' powers. If the destruction of the Vienna system was the price to be paid for demolishing the Treaty of Paris, Russia would be ready to pay that price. In an almost schizophrenic frame of mind Alexander II, by disposition a conservative, particularly in his foreign policy, supported first Napoleon and Cavour, then Bismarck, in their assaults on the Habsburg monarchy. In fact, with the defeat of Russia in the Crimean war, the road was open for every practitioner of the new diplomacy. The three wars that followed, the Italian, the Danish and the Austro-Prussian, were products of revisionist statesmanship. They ended in the almost total discomfiture of the Habsburg monarchy. Indeed after 1867, under the aegis of the former Saxon minister, Beust, Austria herself passed into the revisionist camp. The old order in Europe, set up in 1815 and restored after 1849, was dead.

Yet, though 'the five' had ostensibly achieved their objectives, the new arrangements completed in 1867 did not wholly represent the sum total of their combined ambitions. In fact, 'the contingent and the unforeseen' had entered the arena in the shape of forces operating outside the charmed circle of European chanceries. Not counting the Polish insurrection of 1863, 'popular' forces had erupted three times to disturb their carefully laid designs. On two occasions (in central Italy and Schleswig-Holstein) popular national movements had been skilfully incorporated or deflected into the framework of the new diplomacy. The third movement, Garibaldi's conquest of Southern Italy, provided the occasion for a virtuoso display of Cavour's skill in exploiting revolutionary forces while at the same time posing as a 'saviour' and conservative champion. In fact, however, the movement dislocated the plans of the chanceries, for neither Napoleon III nor Cavour himself had envisaged the united Italy (minus Rome) that had emerged by 1866.

The European order of 1867, fruit of the new diplomacy, had several distinctive features. In the first place, it was the product of force, the result of piecemeal wars deliberately provoked. It was the fruit also of *faits accomplis*, dictated settlements, unilateral or bilateral decisions. The enfeeblement of the 'concert of Europe' had been demonstrated by the ineffectual London Conferences of 1864 on the future of

Schleswig-Holstein. Henceforth, its action would be confined – at least until the Congress of Berlin in 1878 – to the registration of previously negotiated agreements or issues of secondary importance.

Furthermore, in making the new arrangements, the principles of nationality and the consultation of populations to be transferred – except for an insincere obeisance in the case of Nice and Savoy – had been consistently ignored. Conquest alone brought about the inclusion in the new Italy of the *mezzogiorno*. The same was true of the inclusion of various North German territories (e.g. Frankfurt) in the Prussian-dominated North German Confederation. Danish-speakers in North Schleswig were incorporated in the Confederation, notwithstanding Austria's stipulation for a plebiscite in Article V of the Treaty of Prague. In Austria-Hungary the *Ausgleich* of 1867 consecrated unpopular Magyar domination of Croats, Slovaks and Roumanians, as well as the rule of Germans over Czechs in Bohemia. The French-speaking Walloon provinces remained indeed a part of Belgium, but would undoubtedly have been joined to France had Bismarck and Napoleon been able to agree.

Based on force, not principle, the arrangements of 1867 contained few elements of stability. Not a single stable diplomatic alignment survived, except for a largely dynastic (and in part anti-Polish and anti-Napoleonic) entente linking Prussia-North Germany with Russia. With British near-withdrawal from the affairs of the Continent the 'European states system' was in total disarray. Meanwhile pressures for more changes were widespread. While in France nationalist elements craved 'revenge for Sadowa', a party in Vienna longed to reverse the verdict of 1866. The Italians coveted Rome; Russia desired, at the very least, the abolition of the clauses of the Peace of Paris neutralizing the Black Sea.

It was, however, Bismarck who struck the final blow. First he turned down Napoleon III's ambitious proposals for substantial compensation in return for acquiescence in the union of North Germany and the states south of the Main; then he refused to allow the Emperor even the acquisition of Luxemburg. This may be considered the proximate cause of the Franco-Prussian war of 1870. Bismarck's refusal to play the game of diplomacy according to the accepted rules, his decision to 'welsh' on earlier half-promises to Napoleon, ranks – at least in retrospect – among the decisive acts of his political career. It was this, above all, which prevented the consolidation of the European order of 1867 on the basis of a Franco-German balance and shared hegemony, as proposed at one time by Napoleon.

On the reasons for Bismarck's conduct – almost inexplicable on the still widely held assumption that he did not want war with France – it is possible only to speculate. His refusal to agree to the break-up of Belgium might be explained by an unwillingness to antagonize Great Britain, though it is hard to see what her quasi-isolationist government could have done in face of a Franco-Prussian *fait accompli*. But why not allow Napoleon at least the 'consolation prize' of a second Nice and Savoy in the shape of Luxemburg? It is hard to believe that Bismarck was motivated by a German patriotism he almost certainly did not feel (nor, in any case, was Luxemburg essentially 'German'). It is equally improbable that German national sentiment – which he skilfully manipulated whenever required – would have prevented him, had he so desired, from letting the Grand Duchy go to France. If Bismarck was not prepared to contemplate war with France – which in fact he almost certainly was – his conduct can be ascribed only to *hubris*, the arrogance of victory, combined with his openly displayed contempt for the Emperor of the French. Indeed, Prussia's military conventions with the South German States (though no doubt in part defensive), and even more Bismarck's deep involvement in the risky Hohenzollern candidature in Spain suggest, at the very least, a willingness to risk the possibility of war. Moltke for his part ardently desired it and three years later would consider it 'not yet too late'. In fact, the war was expected, sooner or later, by diplomats throughout Europe. It pitted against each other the two powers which, more than any others, had contributed to the destruction of the Vienna system.

The war was engineered and concluded in the spirit of the new diplomacy. It resulted in the incorporation in Germany, against the manifest wishes of the inhabitants, of Alsace and Lorraine. In further unilateral acts, Italian troops occupied Rome, while Alexander II and Gorchakov denounced the Black Sea Clauses. Within a few years, in a violent epilogue, Russia deprived the Ottoman Empire of as much of Bulgaria as the other powers would allow her, with the object of turning it into a satellite principality. Austro-Hungarian forces, in the face of stiff local resistance, occupied Bosnia and Herzegovina. Bismarck, with Austrian assent, freed himself from the obligation to hold a plebiscite in North Schleswig. Finally, the Dual Alliance of 1879 completed and guaranteed the results of the new diplomacy. The cycle of change begun in 1854 was now complete, the new 'post-Vienna' order an accomplished fact.

In the face of the evidence, a persistent liberal-national legend, perpetuated more particularly in Italy and Germany, alleges that the new international order went far towards the application, in accordance with liberal ideas, of the principle of nationality. Nothing could be further from the truth. Though some greatly enlarged national units either came into existence or achieved international recognition, this did not represent primarily a triumph of nationality, let alone liberalism. Wherever questions of nationality inconvenienced the victors, they were curtly brushed aside. As for popular movements, whether national or liberal, these, without exception, were turned into tools of power politics. The 'national' unifications of Italy and Germany resembled nothing so much as conquests by Piedmont and Prussia, with a degree of middle-class and intellectual support and a wider measure of patriotic acquiescence. So far as liberal principles were concerned, these found a place neither in the administration of the Italian *mezzogiorno* (where, indeed, they would have been entirely out of place), nor in the politics of the new German Empire. The anachronistic gesture by which the (reluctant) King of Prussia was proclaimed German Emperor on the proposal of the (unwilling and, indeed, absent) King of Bavaria was a deeply symbolic act.

The new international order, from beginning to end, was the creation of rulers, diplomats, soldiers and bureaucrats. Contrary to their previous practice, the old ruling classes had shown an unwonted assurance and adroitness in manipulating and directing the national movements of the age and in making them serviceable to the purposes of Cabinet diplomacy. Confident statesmen of the new breed, instead of fearing national and liberal movements as their conservative predecessors had done, forced them into accommodations which buttressed their own ascendancy. Indeed, the 'nationalization of nationality' was perhaps their major achievement. Wherever non-official forces had intruded into the process of recasting the map of Europe, they had either been successfully exploited (like Garibaldi's 'Thousand', the anti-Danish movement in Schleswig-Holstein or, arguably, Russian Panslavism in 1876–77) or defeated (like Garibaldi's later raids, the Paris Commune or the Bosnian resistance). Force wielded by governments, not national sentiment, ideology or popular feeling invariably carried the day.

In pursuing the aims of *realpolitik*, governments now disposed of unrivalled resources. They could call on the services of a rapidly advancing technology, of improved communications and of growing reserves of trained manpower. The spread of elementary education, combined with rising literacy, offered growing opportunities for mass indoctrination and the manipulation of opinion – as indeed did peacetime military service and the rapid growth of a newspaper-reading public. The more skilful statesmen, therefore – from Palmerston to Bismarck – could increasingly harness to their purposes the latent emotional resources of nationalism and chauvinism. Propaganda, domestic and international, now became a force to be reckoned with. In face of this growing concentration of power in the hands of governments, the part played by bourgeois leaders in international politics could, in most cases, be at best ancillary.

In fact, international relations to an increasing degree were becoming contests of organized economic resources, including manpower. In war, the economically stronger regularly defeated the less developed. Indeed it would have been virtually impossible for Russia to have conquered England and France in the Crimean war or for Austria to have defeated either France or Prussia. Prussia-Germany, by 1870, had overtaken France in the economic race. Nor was it by accident that the Union forces in the United States finally defeated the Confederacy.

Whether in Italy, the United States or Germany, it was the economically developed North which overcame and imperfectly absorbed the pre-industrial South. Less and less would the outcome of wars be decided by stout hearts (though these would never quite cease to count) or daring cavalry or bayonet charges. Instead, what really mattered would increasingly be trained manpower and railways, advanced armaments, planning and organization. These were not things which could be improvised on the outbreak of war. On the contrary, it was the 'investment' of economic and manpower resources in times of peace that eventually decided the issue, so much so that the outcome of wars might now well be determined before ever a shot was fired. Links between diplomacy and war, industry and domestic politics, were becoming closer. The role of governments, in such matters, was becoming paramount.

58 The Proclamation of the King of Prussia as German Emperor at Versailles. In this deeply symbolic act Bismarck was the central figure, as – in his white uniform – he is in this picture by Anton von Werner.

59, 60 The reality and the glamour: (*above*) crippled British veterans of the Crimean war; (*left*) a somewhat fanciful depiction of the Earl of Cardigan leading the Charge of the Light Brigade before Balaclava.

VIII ARMIES AND SOCIETIES

It was the policy of governments, above all, which determined the forms of military organization. The decades following the overthrow of Napoleon in 1815, in consequence, had been a lean time for Europe's armies. In an age of peace and economic stagnation governments everywhere begrudged every penny of military spending. Prussia's military budget, for example, in 1820 had been 27.5 million thaler, 38 per cent of total expenditure. Almost three decades later (1847) and with an increased population, it was still only 28.3 million thaler, 32 per cent of total spending. Again, while in 1816 the Prussian army had claimed 1.25 per cent of the male population, by 1857 the proportion was only 0.8 per cent.

To the financial stringency of the times the military authorities of different countries had responded in different ways. The French, considered Europe's leading military nation, had concentrated on developing a small professional force of highly trained regulars. The British, by maintenance of the purchase system (which, however, was preserved in the main for other reasons), had ensured that their forces should be in part privately financed. Wealthy cavalry officers contributed from their own pockets to the upkeep of their troops. The Prussian authorities had sought to combine cheapness with a modicum of professional competence through the preservation of a small (and ill-paid) professional nucleus reinforced by a part-time militia, the Landwehr. In Russia, the quest for savings had led through Arakcheev's 'military colonies' to a long-service serf-army maintained at subsistence level. Everywhere, whatever the type of military organization adopted, the desire to cut expense had played a major part.

In more than one army the needs of economy, combined with the absence of major campaigns, had led to an increase of the 'civilian' element. Where ill-paid regular service offered neither adequate financial rewards nor satisfactory career prospects, a premium was placed, on the one hand, on 'part-timers', on the other on courtier-officers. The scanty professional cadres were thus diluted with part-time officers or at the least officers with outside means of support (and, often, civilian interests). A similar trend emerged, more particularly in Prussia, even with regard to NCOs and common soldiers.

This state of affairs was unfavourable to innovation or experiment in the military field. Strategic thinking was dominated by Jomini and Clausewitz, who had gained their military experience in the Napoleonic wars, and from studying the campaigns of Napoleon and Frederick the Great. The more 'modern' Clausewitz, significantly, had stressed the importance of civilian direction of military operations (warfare as a continuation of diplomacy by other means) and the value of a defensive military strategy. Pioneers like the French artillery engineer and inventor Joseph Paixhans had been unable to make headway. Military thinking, bounded by the horizons of Napoleon, Wellington and Blücher (not to mention Suvorov) was backward-looking. Hamstrung by conservative attitudes, military affairs stagnated.

During the long period of peace which followed Waterloo, armies in fact were concerned less with warfare than with politics. From Peterloo to Világos troops everywhere were employed mainly in a variety of police operations. To suppress ill-armed and untrained insurgents, however, did not call for military skills of a high order. The only fighting experience of a more serious kind was acquired in colonial campaigns. This, too, while developing certain special aptitudes, was no preparation for serious continental campaigning. In a time of widespread domestic unrest governments were more conscious of the political than of the military role of armies. In their eyes, the essential quality was not so much military skill as political reliability. Soldiers formed the mainstay of conservative restoration régimes in many parts of Europe. Generals Windischgrätz, Wellington, Paskevich, Radetsky, Cavaignac and Saint-Arnaud, to name only the more important, were prominent defenders of established order. Commanded by men such as these, armies in most major countries had loyally done the bidding of conservative governments.

The Crimean war was the first revelation of the adverse effects on military efficiency of the influences at work since 1815. The British army in particular, in a war which British policy had done much to bring about, showed evidence of an over-all incompetence that contrasted strangely with its achievements of an earlier period. Perhaps its most glaring weakness lay in the inferior quality of its senior com-

61 A Russian serf, about to leave his family for conscript service in the army, being blessed by his father.

manders, most of whom owed their appointments to social connections rather than military skill. Nepotism was widespread among general officers, with Raglan, the commander of the British expeditionary force, appointing no fewer than five of his nephews to his personal staff. On the other hand, of a total of 221 staff officers a mere 15 had passed through the Senior Department of the Royal Military College at Sandhurst. The result of this process of selection attracted the scorn of Lord Wolseley:

> Good Heavens! What Generals then had charge of England's only Army and of her honour and fighting reputation! They were served to a large extent by incompetent staff officers, as useless as themselves, many of them mere 'flaneurs about town', who knew as little about war and its science as they did about the Differential Calculus. Almost all our officers at that time were uneducated as soldiers and many of those placed upon the staff of the Army at the beginning of the war were absolutely unfit for the positions they

had secured through family and political interest. . . . They were not men I would have entrusted with a subaltern's picket in the field. Had they been private soldiers, I don't think any colonel would have made them corporals.

Nor were these strictures excessive. Raglan, comrade in arms, friend and protégé of the Duke of Wellington, had been appointed to command the British expeditionary force at the age of sixty-five. Unable to forget the glories of the Peninsular war, he embarrassed his subordinates by referring to the enemy as 'the French'. His successor, Simpson, was described by Lord Clarendon, the Foreign Secretary, as a 'worthy old gentlewoman', and by the Duke of Newcastle, former Secretary of State for War, as an 'inactive lunatic' who was leading the British army to disaster. Under these commanders, performers like the Earls of Lucan and Cardigan disported themselves. 'We call Lucan the cautious ass and Cardigan the dangerous ass,' wrote one of their subordinates. 'Without mincing matters, two such fools could hardly be picked out of the British army. But they are Earls!' The British cavalry officer, an experienced French officer observed, 'seems to be impressed by the conviction that he can dash or ride over everything; as if the art of war were precisely the same as that of fox-hunting.' 'C'est magnifique, mais ce n'est pas la guerre,' exclaimed an amazed French eyewitness of the Charge of the Light Brigade.

The British command, as it thus presented itself for its first major test since Waterloo, was the product of a number of influences. First and foremost, it was a faithful reflection of British pre-industrial society. It was pervaded by aristocratic prejudice. The Duke, himself an aristocrat, had been a convinced supporter of the purchase system and the privileges of rank. Indeed, one of his major concerns had been to ensure that the officer corps would consist of 'gentlemen'. Recommendations for decorations and distinctions had been reserved for staff officers, usually with aristocratic connections. The claims of regimental officers drawn from a different social background had been systematically ignored. Officers of the Indian Army in particular – the only ones with recent fighting experience – had been consistently snubbed. When the expeditionary force was being assembled, Raglan had given strict orders for applications from 'Indians' to be discouraged. Those who joined nevertheless could be sure of scorn and insult from their well-born 'brother' officers.

The spirit of social exclusiveness thus pervading the British officer corps found its military expression in the prevalent 'cavalry ethos'. A high proportion of generals were in fact drawn from cavalry units. The superior military virtue of cavalry, accordingly, had become established dogma. The reasons were essentially non-military. A cavalry commission signified landed connections, wealth, leisure and horsemanship. It also spelt sartorial elegance. The personal qualities called for, especially in the age of the massed cavalry charge, were dash and a certain type of courage, rather than intelligence or initiative. Service in this élitist arm, moreover, was linked with a haughty arrogance. The man on horseback necessarily looked down on the 'foot-slogger'. Indeed, at the start of the campaign, young cavalry officers in London drawing-rooms were heard to venture the opinion that to take out infantry units to the Crimea would be unnecessary. As they would merely hold back the cavalry, they had better be left at home.

The reasons for the British army cult of the horse were, of course, essentially social. Its function was to ensure the landed amateur status of the British gentleman-officer. The horse, by acting as an instrument of exclusion, guaranteed that the officer corps would be drawn from the ruling class. By the same token it assured the subordination of the military to the civil power. The younger son, 'serving in the army and looking to his elder brother for his hunting and shooting on leave and calculating his chances of succeeding to the estate, would not be a probable participator in a *coup d'état*'. The suicidal Charge of the Light Brigade thus formed part of the insurance premium to be paid for political stability.

Under the command of aristocratic dilettanti, the day-to-day administration of the British army lay in the hands of an economically and socially depressed army bureaucracy. This bureaucracy the Crimean war showed up as 'unreformed', that is routine-ridden, inefficient and chaotic. 'I was never able to distinguish where one department began and another ended,' a witness told the Parliamentary Commission of Enquiry, '. . . through all the departments there was a kind of paralysis, a fear of incurring any responsibility, and a fear of going beyond their instructions.' Florence Nightingale lamented having to work with men 'who are neither gentlemen, nor men of education, nor even men of business, nor men of feeling, whose only object is to keep themselves out of blame'. W. H. Russell, the

133

Times correspondent, indignantly described the treatment of the British soldier under their administration as 'worthy only of the savages of Dahomey'. The system had worked to some extent in peacetime under the supervision of a towering personality like the Duke of Wellington. Now the army had the chastening experience of fighting a major war 'under the system but without the Duke'.

By comparison with its British allies – as, indeed, with the brave but unsophisticated Russians – the French army emerged from the Crimean campaign with its reputation unimpaired. As befitted the forces of a post-aristocratic social system (though not yet an industrial one) it was an army of professionals. Its officers, as a rule, had risen in the service. Most had had comparatively recent fighting experience in Algeria. Generals, on the whole, commanded the loyalty of their subordinates, whose hardships, in large measure, they shared (very unlike that 'noble Yachtsman' the Earl of Cardigan who, with Raglan's permission, spent his nights on his luxury yacht in Balaclava harbour, miles from his cold and hungry troopers, his meals prepared by a French chef). Canrobert in particular showed a real concern for the welfare of his men, regularly visiting the units on horseback. Before the bullet, he assured them, infantry private and general were equal. In consequence, while French morale remained relatively high, French officers attributed many of the troubles that plagued their (often aged) British senior colleagues to their refusal to share the hardships of the rank and file.

'The organisation of the French is beautiful, ours a perfect disgrace,' wrote a British officer, not without exaggeration. It was, in fact, an element of basic professionalism in its organization and approach which played a large part in enabling the French army to outshine the British and to defeat the Russians. French soldiers, moreover, had developed to a high degree the art of improvisation, which they glorified as *le débrouillage*, the *système d.* Their training had made them self-reliant, a characteristic reflected to good purpose also in the relative flexibility of their infantry tactics. In general, French military attitudes, the products of a post-aristocratic society based on the 'career open to talents', reflected, in comparison with the British, very different social attitudes and a very different role of the army in society and tradition.

By the end of the fifties, French military prestige in Europe stood high. While French armies had acquitted themselves with credit both in the Crimea and in Northern Italy, neither the British nor the Russian military reputation had recovered from the Crimean *débâcle*. That of the Austrian armies, notwithstanding their defensive gallantry, had been somewhat tarnished at Magenta and Solferino. As for Prussia, her disorderly mobilization in 1859 merely confirmed the low esteem in which her armed forces were generally held. Their regular cadres were considered, in French military circles, as little better than a training staff for the Landwehr. Nor were their numbers designed to inspire respect. The Landwehr itself, with its civilian militiamen and mainly part-time officers, was held – and the bungled mobilization of 1859 merely confirmed the view – to be ill-trained and lacking in discipline. 'C'est compromettre le métier,' was a French observer's caustic comment on the conduct of the Prussian royal manœuvres in 1861.

The French assessment of Prussian military capabilities agreed in essentials with that of the professional soldier who, in 1858, had assumed the government of Prussia. As early as 1849, the Prince of Prussia had become convinced, both for political and for military reasons, of the need for drastic changes in the Prussian military system. Shortly after assuming the Regency, he received a memorandum written by a high-ranking officer, von Roon. If Prussia was to remain a great power, Roon argued, she would need an 'inexpensive but, at the same time, impressively strong' army. To achieve this, the Landwehr must be integrated more closely with the regular forces. In future, it should be trained as a reserve by regular officers, organized in Area Commands. Men should join it only on completion of seven years' active and regular reserve service. The regular army, including the regular reserves, would comprise seven age groups, while the role of the Landwehr would be reduced to that of a second reserve. More regular officers and NCOs would be needed. To attract suitable recruits, conditions of service must be improved and entry facilitated.

The experience of 1859 lent urgency to Roon's proposals. When the cautiously liberal Minister of War demurred, he was dismissed and Roon appointed in his place. This, in its effects, must rank among the decisive political acts of the century. The appointment as War Minister of an ultra-conservative, a challenge alike to the moderate-liberal ministry of the 'New Era' and to the liberal groups in the Landtag, ushered in an era of constitutional conflict between king and parliament. In 1859 and again in 1860, the Landtag, as a compromise, voted the funds needed for Roon's reforms but in each case for one year only. By 1861, when it finally refused to vote further supplies, the military reorganization had become irreversible. The result was constitutional deadlock, and two successive dissolutions of the Landtag merely served to increase the size of the liberal majority as well as strengthening the determination of the deputies.

Prussia's liberal bourgeoisie was now engaged in what appeared to be a decisive confrontation with the conservative monarchy. By 1862 the King, despairing of success, was contemplating abdication. Roon, as a last desperate expedient, advised the appointment of his political friend and ally Otto von Bismarck as Prime Minister. This was to prove a second decisive act. Under Bismarck's premiership, the government continued to collect taxes – including, of course, those needed to finance the military reforms – on the excuse that the situation which had arisen was not provided for in the Prussian constitution and that the King's government must be carried on. The political crisis Bismarck resolved through a successful foreign policy. Victory over Denmark strengthened the position of the government and weakened the liberal opposition. That of 1866 over Austria ensured the triumph of the Prussian monarchy. An Act of Indemnity passed in 1867 with the votes of a majority of liberal deputies legalized retrospectively the proceedings adopted by the government since 1861. It was the Sedan of Prusso-German liberalism. Henceforth, the defeated bourgeoisie could be, at best, the junior partner of the military and bureaucratic ruling élite.

At no stage of the conflict had the true significance of the constitutional struggle escaped either side in the contest. Two features of Roon's reform highlighted the issues at stake: the virtual destruction of the Landwehr as an autonomous force and the introduction of a three-year period of service. The Landwehr, a citizen force, was a relic of the liberal Prussian reform era of Stein, Hardenberg and Boyen early in the century; as such, it possessed, for Prussian liberals at least, a symbolic value. In 1853, less than a third of its subalterns had been drawn from the nobility – though almost two-thirds of its staff officers (the professional element) were nobles. The Landwehr man, depending on the point of view, could be regarded as either a citizen in arms or a civilian in uniform. In neither capacity did he commend himself to conservative soldiers and politicians. In both, he appealed to the liberals.

The destruction of the old Landwehr would be a severe blow struck at surviving liberal institutions. The second, perhaps more fundamental issue was the extension of the term of military service. Recruits called to the colours had in fact always been liable for three years' service. However, partly for reasons of economy they had normally been sent on indefinite furlough after two years. As two years were not enough for their full 'de-civilianization', they usually left the army as they had entered it, civilians. Combined with the survival of the Landwehr this meant that, at least from the professional soldier's point of view, the 'civilian' elements in the Prussian armed forces had remained disturbingly large. The Landwehr man, Roon complained, did not feel like a soldier. Even when he had learnt something about weapon-handling, 'his soul clung to his farm, his chisel, his work at his home, not to the flag'. This situation Roon, with the Regent's enthusiastic support, proposed to remedy through 'the iron screws of military discipline'.

'Discipline, blind obedience,' the King later contended, 'are things which can be inculcated and made permanent only by long familiarity.' To achieve them, the longer period of service was in his view essential. Indeed, for its supporters, a prime object of the reform was the eradication of the civilian spirit. The 'de-civilianized' army, it was hoped, would become the 'school of the nation'. The officer corps, turning raw recruits into clean and smart soldiers and indoctrinating them with monarchical principles, would counteract the liberal 'poison' of the age. Not only would the army become professionalized. The entire Prussian nation would be permeated with its martial and monarchical spirit.

In fact both supporters and opponents of the reform clearly understood that while enhancing Prussia's military capacity, it was at the same time a deeply political act. While the King chose as his slogan 'a disciplined army, that is also a people in arms, in support of their King and warlord', liberals feared the strengthening of illiberal elements and the formation of a kind of conservative 'party-guard'.

Nor were the social implications of the reform any less clearly apparent. Roon, in his memorandum, had advocated a return to the original concept of the Prussian Cadet Corps as an institution designed primarily to assist impecunious officers and the poorer nobility. With the greater need for regular officers and NCOs, the Corps would now have to be expanded. More generally, the weight of the officer class in society would be increased both through greater numbers and through enhanced prestige. The prime beneficiary of the reform, therefore, would be the Prussian nobility, which, in 1860, not only held a monopoly of Guards commissions but also provided nine-tenths of the cavalry officers. In the infantry, almost three-quarters of the officer corps consisted of nobles though the proportion dropped to less than a third in the artillery where a knowledge of mathematics was required. The higher the rank, the greater the preponderance of nobles. Of generals, nine-tenths in all arms were drawn from the nobility.

In actual fact, somewhat ironically, the expansion resulting from the reform produced at least a temporary dilution. In the sixties, the proportion of non-nobles (sons of petty officials, clergymen, teachers, *rentiers*, merchants and manufacturers) admitted to the Cadet Corps rose to between a quarter and a third of the total, though sons of the commercial bourgeoisie numbered little more than one in twenty. However, irrespective of social background, the Cadet Corps turned all its pupils into professional, authoritarian, monarchist, exclusive and socially conservative officers.

Liberals, as might be expected, protested at the transformation of the hitherto partly 'open' officer corps into an 'exclusive special caste, the first estate in the country'. But, while recognizing the social implications of the reform, they were ready, at least in their majority, to pay even this price for the attainment of patriotic objectives. In the face of Bismarck's diplomatic successes the bulk of liberals readily resigned themselves to the social and political consequences of the reform. With liberal consent, the Prussian social system, as well as the political, was frozen, largely through the new military organization, in a mainly conservative mould.

Ironically, among the causes contributing to this result, not the least had been Prussia's growing prosperity. This logically should, if anything, have strengthened the liberals in their struggle with the monarchy. In fact, it benefited mainly the latter. In the event, not only did prosperity facilitate the introduction of the reform, but it also helped to finance Bismarck's wars. Yet the reforms, originally, had been introduced in conditions of recession for it was not until 1861 that the Prussian economy recovered fully from the crisis of 1857. Indeed financial considerations had been prominent in the arguments of the opposition. The reforms, it was thought, would add roughly a

62 Boys of the Prussian Cadet Corps. Though Roon's reforms temporarily diluted the social exclusiveness of the Corps with the sons of the bourgeoisie, the end product was still professional, conservative and authoritarian.

third (10 million thaler a year) to the military budget. The burden, liberals argued, would prove ruinous. The government countered by pointing to the sound state of Prussian finances. Even with the reform, it claimed, the proportion of net revenue absorbed by military expenditure would remain the lowest of any major country.

Moreover, to make the reform less unpalatable to the liberals and, at the same time, reduce the traditional under-taxation of rural areas, the Prussian government, in 1861, resolved to raise the extra revenue needed mainly from landed property. In fact, it had decided to combine military reorganization with a major tax reform. A feature of the land-tax as levied hitherto had been its grossly uneven distribution not only as between different provinces but even within the same province. No fewer than twenty major systems of assessment were in operation. Extensive historic immunities survived. Now rates and procedures would be standardized. This would help to raise the bulk of the 10 million thaler a year needed for Roon's reform. Moreover, by shrewdly playing off liberals against conservatives, the government succeeded in rationalizing the business tax as well, making it more profitable in the process. Though the implementation of the land-tax reform was postponed until 1863, pending the compilation of new tax registers, the financing of military reform was thus assured.

The new tax arrangements were soon proved to have been hardly even necessary. With the upsurge of the economy in 1861, revenue from indirect taxation (well over half the total) as well as income from state enterprises rose sharply. Whereas a deficit of 3.5 million thaler had been anticipated in the budget for 1861, an unexpected surplus of 5 million thaler emerged. More than half the extra revenue had come from state domains and forests, railways, mines and postal services, most of the rest from indirect taxation.

The buoyancy of the revenue continued. In 1863, the reformed land-tax was collected. For the year 1865, the accounts, once again, bore witness to the highly favourable state of the Prussian finances. Revenue, compared with the previous year, had increased by more than 7 million thaler. The land and buildings tax yielded an extra 3 million, while the proceeds of indirect taxation had risen by almost 2 million. More than 7.5 million thaler were now available for 'new expenditures and the increase of existing ones', for improvements in communications, the advancement of science and education, and supplying the needs of war veterans. Growing prosperity, by helping to finance not only the military reforms but also Bismarck's wars, confounded the gloomy prophecies of the liberals and robbed them of their credibility. It strengthened the hand of the government. Ironically, the very success of the Prussian bourgeoisie in the economic sphere contributed to its political discomfiture.

In France, in analogous circumstances, it was the bourgeoisie which carried the day. In fact, what the mobilization of 1859 had been to Prussia, the Prussian victory over Austria at Sadowa was to France. Just as the former event had convinced the Prince Regent of the urgent need for military reform, so the latter jolted Napoleon III. The French Emperor even found his Roon in the person of Marshal Niel. In Paris, as in Berlin, liberals in the Chambers opposed increased military expenditure on financial as well as political grounds. There are analogies also between the effects of economic depression in Prussia after 1857 and in France after 1867. In each case, the result was a conflict between monarchy and Lower Chamber. The outcomes of the two conflicts, however, differed widely with important consequences for Europe.

In November 1866, under the impact of Sadowa, Napoleon convened a conference of his military advisers at Compiègne. It was then estimated in French military circles that the Prussian army, when fully mobilized, could muster a strength of 1,200,000 trained men as against the French army's 300,000. Napoleon therefore set his advisers the target figure of one million men. One school of thought, to which he himself inclined, favoured the Prussian model. A large trained reserve should be created through universal short-term service. Against this view, conservatives led by Randon, the Minister of War, argued in favour of lengthening service with the colours, if necessary to nine years. Randon, true to the traditional view of the French army, doubted the military value of reservists. Other arguments put forward by civilian members of the conference concerned the loss of manpower which might have serious effects on French agriculture. Prefectorial reports indicated that any new military impositions would be desperately unpopular with both commercial interests and the peasantry. With an election approaching this would be a serious matter for the weakening imperial régime. In the face of conflicting viewpoints the Compiègne discussions ended in deadlock.

At this point Marshal Niel drew up a plan resembling in more than one respect Roon's memorandum of 1859. The Garde Nationale, the Marshal proposed, disbanded after Napoleon's coup in 1851, should be reconstituted. Its functions, roughly, should be those of the new Prussian Landwehr. Niel's was a compromise proposal. Under it, the practice of calling up each year small contingents for the regular forces would be continued. Recruits would serve six years, thus maintaining the traditional professional nucleus. Those not called up for regular service, on the other hand, would receive intensive military training with the Garde, and so would regulars on completion of their service. By this means an army of over 800,000 would eventually be built up, reinforced by 400,000 Gardes Mobiles. This, it was held, would match the Prussian forces. Napoleon accepted the proposals. When Randon demurred, arguing that what France needed was soldiers, not recruits, he was dismissed – as Bonin had been dismissed in Prussia in 1859 – and replaced by Niel. Niel's proposals were laid before the legislature. Military reform had become a question of political will.

The Conseil d'Etat, a body of cautious bureaucrats, proposed the reduction of colour service to five years, to be supplemented by four years in the regular reserve. The training proposed for men called up for the Garde would be only minimal. When these proposals were presented to the legislature, Thiers argued that the 30 million francs earmarked for the Garde would be better spent on expanding the regular army. Imperialist deputies, preoccupied with electoral considerations, feared that the proposals would be desperately unpopular in the country. The bourgeois would lose the possibility of 'buying out' his son, either by paying a substitute or by contributing to a fund to supplement the pay of re-enlisting regulars. The peasant's son would lose the possibility of total exemption through drawing a *bon numéro* in the annual ballot. From the left came pleas for the total disbandment of the regular army and its replacement by a Swiss-style militia. 'Do you want to turn France into a barracks?' shouted Jules Favre, interrupting a speech by Niel. 'As for you,' the Marshal retorted, 'take care that you don't turn it into a cemetery.'

In opposing the Niel reform the Chamber accurately reflected the views of the electorate. Official reports from the provinces agreed that the peasantry, the mainstay of the imperial régime, feared the loss of its *bons numéros*, besides expressing concern at the shortage of manpower on the land. Industrialists and representatives of *haut commerce*, alarmed at the proposed suppression of *exonération* and anxious about possible fiscal burdens, signed petitions against the proposals. A provincial official reported 'egotism of the well-to-do classes, fears of the agricultural populations'. Emotive arguments were circulating. The Procureur-général of Dijon was not alone in considering the Prussian model 'an almost barbarous system, incompatible with the customs, the education and the fortune of a great nation'. His colleague in Besançon declared that 'the mere thought of a possible imitation of the Landwehr affronts our customs, so jealous of liberty and independence.' In fact, among the political classes there existed a genuine fear that the proposed 'militarization' of the nation might presage a return to authoritarian government. There was reluctance also to furnish the régime with forces for further military adventures like the one approaching its inglorious conclusion in Mexico.

In the face of mounting opposition in the country, of which deputies, anxious for their seats, made themselves the spokesmen, Napoleon and Niel, both sick men, retreated step by step and against their better judgment. Finally, a sadly truncated reform emerged from the debates of the Chamber early in 1868. A contingent of conscripts would, as hitherto, be selected by ballot each year to serve for five years with the colours and four in the reserve. A further contingent would serve for five months only. Those who escaped the call-up would serve during a period of five years in the Garde Mobile. They would be called up for fourteen days in the year (Niel had pleaded for a minimum of three weeks), not more than one day at a time and not more than twelve hours in a day (to enable them to return to their homes the same night). The *rapporteur* reporting the Bill to the Chamber had argued that there would be enough time for training while the Garde was being mobilized. Less hypocritically, an imperialist deputy explained: 'We have got to vote this law as the Emperor wants it, but we'll fix it so that it can't work.' And that, indeed, is what happened. The Garde Mobile never fully materialized. The Chamber was determined to economize. Even Niel's modest proposal at least to reduce the number of men on permanent furlough was vetoed on grounds of expense.

In trying to create an army capable of matching that of Prussia, Niel was swimming against the tide – as was his imperial master. Worn out prematurely, Niel died in 1869. His successor, Lebœuf, popular in the legislature, tried to work with the parliamentary majority. The deputies, inspired by pacifist sentiments and the desire to economize, consistently pared down military appropriations. The proportion of men on furlough was increased. At the end of June 1870, a fortnight before the outbreak of war (which French public opinion did not a little to provoke), the Ollivier ministry proposed a reduction of the annual contingent by 10,000 men. Members of the opposition argued that the military burden was becoming intolerable. An arms race would lead to war. France's armaments were a provocation to her peaceful neighbours. Even Thiers, oppositionist though he was, was provoked into declaring that 'to talk of disarmament in the present state of Europe one needs to be both foolish and ignorant'. Lebœuf desperately drew attention to the menace beyond the Rhine. Napoleon wrote a pamphlet, *Une Mauvaise Economie*, in which he compared the military strengths of France and Germany. Ignoring a personal appeal, the deputies cut the military budget by another 13 million francs. By this time, it hardly mattered.

When war came, the failure of the Niel reform had put France at a decisive disadvantage in respect of trained manpower. Her military strength was less than half that of Germany. The Garde Mobile existed largely on paper. The few units that were embodied were ill-disciplined and militarily useless. Thanks to the failure of Napoleon and Niel, the French army was decisively outnumbered.

In France, unlike Prussia, the parliamentary opposition had defeated the government on the issue of military reform. Civilians, to a large extent, had carried the day against the soldiers. But there was a price to be paid for their victory. Imperialist, Orleanist and Radical, bour-geois, peasant, intellectual and worker together went down in com-mon and resounding defeat. In the military sphere at any rate, the system of William I, Roon and Moltke had been triumphantly vindicated.

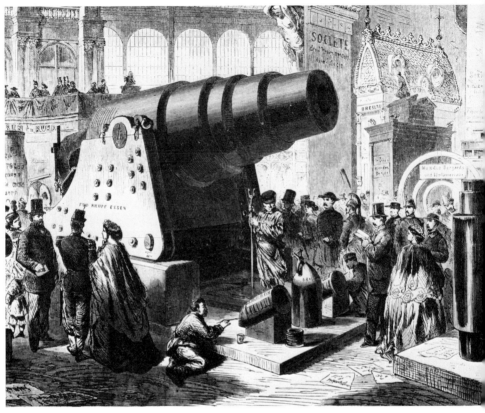

63, 64 The sinews of war. (*Above*) Krupps' thousand-pounder 14-inch siege-gun, shown at the Paris Universal Exhibition of 1867; (*below*) part of the Whitworth armaments factory: bas-relief on the statue of Sidney Herbert in Waterloo Place, London.

IX THE SINEWS OF WAR

Though France in 1870 was outnumbered on the field of battle, her defeat was not exclusively, indeed not even primarily, attributable to her inferiority in trained manpower. New factors, reflecting the broader developments in society, were coming into play. Perhaps the most important was the application in the military field of progressive industrial technology. Industrialists like Whitworth, Armstrong or Alfred Krupp produced (sometimes also designed) weapons of unprecedented effectiveness. Guns and shells of every kind gained greatly in range, accuracy and power of impact. The iron-clad and its successor the iron battleship replaced the wooden ships of the line, steam succeeded sail, screw and propeller the paddle. The introduction of the gun-turret ushered in a revolution in naval tactics. In fact, both pace and scope of innovation in the sphere of military technology during the period exceeded anything hitherto seen. While the Crimean campaign was still fought essentially with the weapons and tactics of the Napoleonic era, the Franco-Prussian war (anticipated in some respects by the American Civil War) could be described as Europe's first 'modern', that is, technological and industrial, war.

Technological change applied to military matters had important social effects. The introduction of improved weapons and new techniques increased the role of the trained specialist, above all of the mathematics-based engineer or artilleryman. Understanding the mechanism of a gun or a battleship was becoming a more important skill than familiarity with the dispositions of a horse. It was symbolic that the only commander to acquit himself with real credit during the Crimean war was Totleben, the Russian engineer general who organized the defence of Sevastopol. In the navies, the introduction of steam increased the importance of the engineer officer afloat.

In general, the impact of science and technology on warfare put a premium on specialization, on intellect and on a new kind of technical expertise. Everywhere, moreover, those best equipped to exploit the new technology came in the main from social backgrounds differing from that of the traditional officer corps. Whatever the resistance put up by men of the 'old school', the emergence of a new type of officer was an inevitable consequence of the mechanization of warfare. Even the British Royal Navy, stronghold of social conservatism, was obliged, in the face of fierce opposition, to improve the status of the engineer officer afloat. Nor was the change confined to the officer class only. Service in gun–crew or battleship required, even of NCO and common soldier (or sailor), mechanical aptitudes and a degree of literacy found more commonly among 'machine-minders' than among those taken from the plough. Though the age of the machine-gunner still lay in the future, the skills of the mechanic were acquiring a growing relevance to the art of war.

The new complexities of warfare, moreover, increasingly called for new techniques of military organization. Staff-work, as the Prussian command in particular would prove, was becoming, to an extent unparalleled in the past, an essential ingredient of the art of war. The need was emerging for a type of officer combining tactical training of a high order with some of the skills of industrial organization and management. After Moltke, the staff officer everywhere would be no longer a hunting aristocrat but a highly trained administrator and something of an intellectual to boot. He would have to combine an aristocratic ethos, essential for reasons of *esprit de corps* and discipline, with many of the qualities of a successful civil servant. And whatever the resentment felt by the traditional officer caste, it was obliged to accept the new breed of staff officer as well as the new technical expert. It was no accident that three commoners with a commercial background, Cardwell, Childers and Goschen, between them gave the British armed forces their modern administrative shape. The modernization of the Russian army following the Crimean *débâcle* was the work of Totleben, a military engineer, and Dmitri Miliutin, an intellectual turned administrator who had started his career as an artillery instructor. In France those chiefly concerned with military reform were Napoleon, an amateur with a life-long interest in artillery matters, and Niel, another military engineer.

The armed forces, in short, and the art of war itself, were coming to be linked more closely to the progress of industrial technology. The growing employment of increasingly pure, resistant and malleable varieties of iron and steel affected not only construction, machine-building, traction and navigation but also weapons and tactics.

Industrialists were beginning to adapt their new inventions to the service of war. The Krupps, originally concerned mainly with the manufacture of axles and weldless steel tyres for railways, increasingly applied their steel smelting and casting skills to the production of superior field-guns and howitzers. The market for their products became world-wide, with Russia, thanks largely to the foresight of Totleben, among their earliest customers. The turning-point in Krupp's career as an arms manufacturer came with the first Prussian order for 300 cast-steel barrels for field-guns secured in 1859 thanks to the personal intervention of the Prince Regent. In much the same way William Armstrong, designer and manufacturer of hydraulic cranes and accumulators, turned his attention to the design and production of ordnance under the impact of the Crimean war. A gun of novel design produced by him in 1859 has been described as 'the first truly modern weapon'. Between 1859 and 1863 Armstrong, rewarded with a knighthood, served as Director of Rifled Ordnance at the Royal Arsenal, Woolwich. Following his return to his own engineering works on the Tyne, he devoted himself to the production of ever larger and more sophisticated ordnance.

Perhaps even more significant than Armstrong was another industrialist, Joseph Whitworth. Born at Stockport in 1803, Whitworth, on leaving school at the age of fourteen, was sent to an uncle's mill to study cotton-spinning. Partly in consequence of his experience with machinery at the mill, he decided to become a machine-builder. From 1821 to 1833 he was employed as a craftsman-mechanic with a succession of machine-manufacturers in the Manchester and London areas. On returning to Manchester, he set up his own workshop. His experience as a craftsman had impressed him with the overriding need for exact measurement and accurate workmanship. He had, in fact, devised new methods for achieving these, which he now proceeded to put into practice. From modest beginnings, his works grew rapidly.

At the Great Exhibition of 1851, Whitworth's exhibits received high commendations. They included, characteristically, a millionth-part measuring machine. During the Crimean war, the government consulted Whitworth on the re-equipment of the Enfield Royal Small Arms factory. His thoughts, in consequence, turned to the manufacture of arms. To this task he brought, above all, his unprecedented standards of precision. Where previously manufacturers had worked in fractions of inches, Whitworth operated in terms of thousandths and even ten-thousandths. The rifle he designed after many experiments proved, not surprisingly, the most accurate available. Only the smallness of its bore delayed its adoption until 1869. Characteristically much of Whitworth's attention, in his later years, was devoted to the improvement of technical education and to bringing it within reach of members of the artisan class. Numerous scholarships he endowed, as well as laboratories he financed at Owen's College in Manchester, testify to his interest. Whitworth's career, with its emphasis on invention and design, on craftsmanship, precision, standardization (particularly of screw threads), education and philanthropy, made him the model of the Smilesian engineer. It was also characteristic of the age in linking industry, technology and armaments. Indeed, were an attempt made to select the representative British public figure of the age, few, besides Joseph Paxton, would have a stronger claim than the industrious and inventive Northerner upon whom Queen Victoria, fittingly, bestowed a baronetcy in 1869.

A characteristic feature of the growing armaments industry was the close link between invention, design and production. Alfred Krupp, for instance, already the head of a world-famous enterprise, himself designed down to the last detail the great fifty-ton hammer 'Fritz' which, after 1861, made his forge one of the most up to date in Europe. No less significant was the contribution of Henry Bessemer. A self-taught engineer, son of a type-founder, Bessemer's early interest lay in the development of electro-typing and the improvement of type-setting machinery. Meanwhile, he earned a small fortune by devising a secret process for the manufacture of 'gold' powder for making 'gold' paint. As with Armstrong and Whitworth, it was the Crimean war, the nursery of British arms technology, which turned Bessemer's thoughts to weapons manufacture. His contribution in the first place consisted of a novel rotating artillery shell. On discovering that the cast-iron cannon then in use were too weak to fire it, he set out to seek a stronger material. In 1856, the Bessemer process for the decarburization of molten pig-iron was announced, producing an extremely malleable mild steel. Following early difficulties, it came to be widely used after 1864. Presently enormous quantities of Bessemer steel went into the building of bridges, railways and ships. The new steel thus was, in fact, an industrial by-product of Bessemer's venture into the field of weapons technology.

Other engineer-inventor-industrialists similarly helped, at any rate incidentally, to promote the manufacture of arms. Thus William (later Sir William), brother of the better-known Werner Siemens, an electrical engineer, pioneered the Siemens-Martin method of heating air supplied to blast-furnaces. The process, shown at the Paris Exhibition of 1867, supplemented and advanced the work of Bessemer. In the Ruhr the young August Thyssen, whose rolling-mill started production in 1867, inaugurated in 1871, through the firm of Thyssen and Co., the process of vertical integration linking iron and coal-mining with steel-making and the production of armour plate and other military materials. In addition, therefore, to serving civil needs, heavy industry, in several countries, was becoming increasingly involved in arms production.

The association of technology and industry with armaments, exemplified in the careers of men like Krupp, Armstrong, Bessemer and Whitworth, illustrates the growing connection between warfare and 'heavy industry'. Increasingly, military efficiency was seen to require a sound industrial and technological base. Some industrial enterprises in their turn, were to a growing extent becoming geared to, if not dependent upon, orders for military equipment. Such orders were on the increase for a number of reasons, including the growing size of armies. French arsenals, for instance, within a few years produced a million Chassepôt rifles. Technological advances in armaments necessitated periodic re-equipment. While rapid-firing weapons increased the consumption of ammunition, losses of *matériel* caused by successive wars created the need for replacements.

A number of factors thus combined to increase military demands on industry. Military orders in their turn became a stimulus to invention as well as investment, expansion and mass production. An international arms market also developed with Krupps in Essen and Vickers-Armstrong in England among the more prominent suppliers. Everywhere, links were being forged between governments, military establishments and heavy industry. Bismarck, for instance, for military reasons, encouraged Thyssen's vertical integration. Meeting the growing requirements of the armed forces, in all major countries, became an increasingly significant aspect of industrial activity.

One consequence of greater technological sophistication in the military field was the growing costliness – at least in absolute terms – of armed forces, whether in peace or war. This did not necessarily mean that military expenditure absorbed a larger share of national resources. Indeed, the surprising ease with which Prussia financed her military expansion and France not only recuperated from the Franco-Prussian war but also raised a huge indemnity, suggests that, at least so long as prosperity lasted, the growth of resources on the whole kept pace with if it did not exceed that of military expenditure.

Meanwhile, the rising cost and sophistication of weapons and organization, the new speed of movement and mobility of forces and the intensification of international rivalries turned military matters, to an unprecedented degree, into peacetime preoccupations. With the growing need for speedy mobilization, up-to-date weaponry and different kinds of expertise, old haphazard methods and 'Crimea-style' improvisation in emergencies receded into the past. Little, now, could safely be left to the last minute. Instead, the outcome of battles and campaigns would depend more and more on peacetime preparation. Governments realized that meticulous planning and organization, superimposed on a strong industrial and educational base, might make the difference between victory and defeat. In consequence, thinking on many matters – the siting of railway lines is a case in point – was influenced increasingly by strategic considerations. After the Prussian victories of 1866 and 1870, thinking on matters of public policy was greatly influenced by military considerations. When W. E. Forster introduced his Education Bill in England in 1870, for instance, one of his arguments was that an educated nation could provide better soldiers. In France, too, compulsory primary education – an education with a high patriotic content – was called for after 1871 on military grounds. Sadowa, it was widely considered, had been a victory for the Prussian schoolmaster. Indeed, with every new war, increasing forethought and resources would now be invested in preparation for the next. Militarism was becoming self-sustaining.

In all these ways, war and the preparation for war were changing their character under the impact of technological advance. Both, in effect, were being invested with a new bourgeois rationality. Though the Ruskins, Carlyles and Burckhardts were slow to realize it, warfare was rapidly losing its romantic aspect, its glamour and most of the primitivism associated with individual 'valour' and 'manly virtues'. Instead, the 'art' of war, in keeping with the general character of the age, was assuming a 'colder', more scientific aspect. While it did not become wholly a matter of machines, it became more mechanical and controlled. The Crimean war had been something of an insane 'hit and miss' adventure, a game of 'blind-man's buff', befitting a pre-scientific age. The Franco-Prussian war on the other hand, only fifteen years after the fall of Sevastopol, showed distinct elements of rationality, of intelligent planning and purposeful control – at least on the part of the victors. Neither side, as the major engagements showed, had yet wholly abandoned the archaic cavalry charge reminiscent of Balaclava. But the Chassepôt of St Privat-Gravelotte, no less than Krupp's ubiquitous field-gun, proved itself an effective weapon. Even if the war of 1870 still contained archaic elements (apart, of course, from the inevitable incidence of chance and human fallibility) it is impossible to overlook the remarkable changes that occurred, as part of the wider movement of the age, between the siege of Sevastopol and that of Paris, the battle of Balaclava and the battle of Sedan.

The Crimean war, coming as it did after decades of peace, had drawn attention to the military shortcomings of all the combatants. The British and Russian military systems were revealed as 'archaic', reflecting the character of semi-feudal rather than industrial societies. The French system, based on attenuated Napoleonic traditions and the experience of colonial warfare in Algeria, had proved its superiority only in relative terms. Among the lessons taught by the war had been the importance of organization. It was not least the quality of its commissariat, its catering, supply and medical services, which had enabled the French expeditionary forces – unlike the British – to weather the cruel winter of 1854–55 in relatively good shape. Yet even the professionalism of the French *troupier* and soldier of fortune, which so impressed the British, had been based on little more than a glorified pragmatism.

The Crimean war, little more than a magnified colonial campaign, provided an opportunity for French administration to shine, at least by comparison with rudimentary Russian organization or the British 'system without the Duke'. The limitations of French staff-work, however, were revealed only too plainly in 1859 in face of the un-familiar task of detraining large bodies of troops and equipment. Provision of the necessary facilities had proved beyond the imagina-tive grasp of senior staff officers in Paris. Nor, despite warnings from several quarters, did the French staff prove capable of appreciating the potential of Krupp's new field ordnance. Until 1870, its major occupation was the collection of military information and the pro-duction of maps – of Germany. That a campaign might actually be fought on French soil was a possibility outside its imaginative range.

Yet the Crimean war had in fact initiated a revolution in the techniques of staff-work. Moltke, appointed Chief of the Prussian General Staff in 1857, drew his conclusions from the spectacle of Crimean fumbling. On taking up his post, he had found Prussian military organization in routine-ridden decay. By 1870 he fashioned, in the shape of the new Prusso-German General Staff, an instrument perfectly adapted to the task of directing the mobilization, dispersed movement and military operations of a modern mass army. The secret of Moltke's success lay characteristically less in any profound originality of concepts or broad imaginative sweep than in hard work, determination, clarity of thought and meticulous attention to detail.

Moltke's new-style staff officer was the product of the most rigorous 'natural selection' and 'survival of the fittest'. Aspirants were drawn exclusively from the ranks of outstanding graduates of the Prussian Military Academy. Twelve of a class of forty (itself recruited from a hundred and twenty applicants) were admitted to the privilege of being trained under the eye of the Chief of Staff. Whoever failed to meet his exacting requirements was returned at once to regimental duties. It was the single-minded selection of an expert professional élite. Trainee officers, moreover, were not future intellectuals operat-ing in a remote military 'think-tank'. Before every step in their promotion, the future staff officers would serve for a period with regiments of the line. This gave them not only practical service experience, but also invaluable contact with regimental officers and men. It also enabled them to function at the same time as Moltke's 'missionaries', working for the gradual conversion of the army to his own professional views.

The tactical training to which Moltke subjected his pupils was attuned to the needs of the new-style mass army emerging from Roon's military reforms. It took full account of the role of railways, particularly during mobilization. It was also geared to the imple-mentation of his tactical concept of 'marching separately and fighting jointly'. Particular attention was given – to good effect, as the cam-paign of 1870 would show – to the problem of co-ordinating the operations of dispersed military units. Emphasis was also laid on the organization of supplies in conditions of rapid movement. In general,

65 Moltke in his office at General Staff HQ in Berlin.

acting as a nerve centre for the Prussian armies, Moltke's staff was trained to ensure the relatively smooth, speedy, co-ordinated and purposeful movement of large, complex and potentially unwieldy armies. Efficient staff-work and control facilitated, without excessive chaos or dislocation, changes in strategy to meet evolving situations. It was largely the work of the staff which lay behind the fact – the importance of which it is difficult to exaggerate – that while French troops on campaign, when operating in large formations, moved at a rate of five or six miles a day, the Prussians were accustomed to marching fifteen. Without an organization of the kind created by Moltke, large numbers in the field, as the French would learn to their cost, could be a liability rather than an asset.

Not that Moltke's staff was composed of 'supermen'. Serious short-comings, revealed both in 1866 and 1870, attest the contrary. On the other hand, the Prussian staff, alert, flexible and self-critical, had the ability to learn from its mistakes. On its superiority over every rival, contemporaries were agreed. Austrian staff-work both before and during the decisive battle of Sadowa was deplorable. The efforts of Colonel Stoffel, the observant French Military Attaché in Berlin, to alert the French command to the part played by the Prussian General Staff in the victory of 1866 proved vain. Military opinion in Paris resented all suggestion of changes in the venerably ineffectual Corps d'Etat Major. French mobilization in the summer of 1870, therefore, was unavoidably chaotic. The promising Central Commission on Military Movement by Railway, set up by Niel in 1869, had been forced to suspend its activities after some useful preparatory work. It had fallen victim to the cost-cutting proclivities of the Corps législatif and to the traditionalism of the French military mind with its professed faith in *morale* and *élan* (sufficient for victory in the Crimea and – barely – in northern Italy).

Moltke's staff, on the other hand – it had the advantage of six railway lines to the frontier to France's two – had, predictably, planned its mobilization down to the last detail. The result was what might have been expected. Germany, within the space of eighteen days, mobilized 1,183,000 troops, regulars and reservists. Within little over a fortnight 462,000 men stood poised on the frontiers of France. French mobilization, on the other hand, out of chaos, produced some 200,000 men (Lebœuf had expected 385,000) at the end of the first fortnight. Some days later, out of 230,000 troops assembled, less than 200,000 were operative. In the circumstances, all thought of an offensive strategy had perforce to be abandoned. The efficiency of German mobilization combined with French deficiencies to ensure that the great war for the military mastery of Europe would be fought on French soil.

The Prusso-Germans revealed their superiority in armaments and tactics, no less than in staff-work. Weapon development since 1855 had been rapid. Although the Crimean war itself made little direct contribution to the development of either armaments or tactics, important conclusions were drawn from the Crimean experience. The destruction of the Turkish squadron at Sinope in 1853, set on fire by Russian incendiary shells, sounded the death-knell of the old wooden ship of the line. Shortly before the end of the war, moreover, the French had introduced 'floating batteries' for the bombardment of the Russian base of Kinburn. These were small, cut-down wooden vessels lined with iron plates fastened to a wall of timber. Russian round-shot bounced off them. The French, it appeared, had found the answer to incendiary shells. In 1858, they went on to lay down the first armour-plated battleship, *La Gloire*. Great Britain, after some initial hesitation, replied with the completely iron *Warrior*. From

1861, no battleship was built of anything other than iron until, in the mid-eighties, iron in its turn was superseded by steel.

The experience of the Crimean war produced other important results. It was during 1855 that the British government first called on the services of Armstrong and Whitworth who, in the years that followed, proceeded to transform British armaments. In general, the Crimean war convinced engineers that shell was capable of improvement. Both the modern shell and the modern gun soon appeared, almost simultaneously. Weapons now carried further, were more accurate and had a greater power of penetration than before. Artillery was being revolutionized.

In infantry fighting, the state of weaponry and hence of tactics appeared to favour the offensive. The Russians, in the first Crimean engagement, had been driven by the Allies from their seemingly impregnable position beyond the river Alma. At Solferino five years later a furious charge of the French Guards swept away the defending Austrian riflemen before they could deploy their full fire-power. In 1864, German infantry stormed the Danish fortifications at Düppel. Two years later the Prussian Guards, at Sadowa, captured the strategic heights of Chlum. Rifle-fire, seemingly, was incapable of stopping determined infantry attack.

Yet, notwithstanding the Prussian success at Chlum, the battle of Sadowa had, in fact, re-established the rifleman's defensive superiority. When, misled by the experience of Solferino, Austrian infantry tried to emulate the *furore franchese*, they were stopped short by the fire of the Prussian needle-gun. The attackers were decimated. Yet, surprisingly, the needle-gun was not a new weapon at all. The Dreyse gun, a breech-loading rifle, had been introduced in the Prussian army as early as 1843. It had not, however, revealed its full potential until Sadowa. Now Prussian soldiers, able to reload in a prone position, were able to fire six shots to every one of their adversaries'. Defence, it seemed, was again in the ascendant.

The French military authorities, including Napoleon, pondering the lessons of Sadowa, reached the obvious – though not necessarily correct – conclusion that it was primarily the Prussian needle-gun that had decided the issue. To restore the military balance, therefore, the French army must be equipped with a weapon of at least comparable performance. This was the long-awaited opportunity of M. Chassepôt, an employee in one of the state arsenals who, without official encouragement, had for years been experimenting with a new breech-loading rifle. Its distinctive feature was a rubber ring for sealing the breech, a device designed to prevent the escape of gas. This, while giving the rifle a longer range, also made it easier and safer to fire. Whereas the Dreyse gun, the presumptive victor of Sadowa, had a range of 600 yards, Chassepôt's weapon was sighted up to 1,600. Its small calibre, moreover, allowed the infantryman to carry extra ammunition. Chassepôt's, in fact, was far and away the best rifle in the field. Though its prototype had been available since 1863, the French military authorities had hesitated to adopt it. Chassepôt's rifle, the traditionalists argued, would waste ammunition. They had constantly demanded further tests, while professing to await the arrival of a still more perfect weapon. Under the impact of Sadowa, however, Napoleon overruled the opposition, ordering the Chassepôt rifle to be put into immediate production. When war came in 1870, a million Chassepôts were in service. The Prussians, on the other hand, were caught by the war before they had carried out the planned re-equipment of their infantry. In infantry weapons, at any rate, the French, thanks to Chassepôt's invention (and Napoleon's determination), enjoyed a clear superiority.

They had, moreover, for a decade been developing a further 'secret' weapon. This was the *mitrailleuse*, the first automatic or 'machine' gun. Composed of a bundle of twenty-five barrels, detonated successively by turning a handle, it was capable of firing 150 rounds a minute up to a range of 2,000 yards. This was a weapon the Prussians feared. A potential 'winner', like the Chassepôt, it was put into production in 1866. However, the secrecy surrounding the *mitrailleuse* was such as to prevent all tactical study of its operation, let alone the training of personnel. When the test came, faulty tactical deployment in bunched batteries with fixed sighting at maximum range impeded its effectiveness. French hopes and Prussian fears alike were proved unjustified.

Ironically, despite the apparent technological advantage of the French it was neither Chassepôt nor *mitrailleuse* that in the event proved the 'winner'. Instead the true 'secret weapon' of the Franco-Prussian war was the Prussian light field-gun. Prussian artillery, at Sadowa, had performed disappointingly. Its park, a mixture of new rifled breech-loaders and obsolete smooth-bores, had been faultily deployed under Corps command some distance from the fighting line. Some of Krupp's cast-steel field-guns, moreover, had developed

66 Prussian field-gun, 1870.

67 The Chassepôt rifle in action.

serious technical defects. The honours, if anything, had gone to the
Austrian gunners. The Prussian authorities, however, had drawn the
proper conclusions. After 1866, under a little-known officer who,
nevertheless, may have changed the face of history, they set about
improving their artillery. General of Artillery von Hindersin,
appointed to the new post of Inspector-General of Artillery, super-
vised the re-equipment of the Prussian batteries with improved cast-
steel breech-loading field-guns, the stars of the Essen stable. Subse-
quently a new school of gunnery trained gun-crews to hitherto
undreamt-of standards of speed and accuracy.

The French, in the meantime, had drawn from the undistinguished
performance of the Prussian artillery at Sadowa the comforting
conclusion that improvements in their own gun-park were not a
matter of urgency. The conversion to breech-loading of the rifled
muzzle-loaders introduced in 1858 would be costly. They had, moreover, proved their worth in the Italian campaign. It is true that French
officers attending the Belgian royal manœuvres in 1867 reported
urgently on the superior range and accuracy of Krupp's steel breech-
loaders. And Krupp himself, at the time of the Paris Exhibition of
1867, respectfully drew the attention of the French authorities to the
quality of his products. But prolonged bureaucratic delays on the

French side reinforced opposition from traditionalists who distrusted the use of steel (French guns were cast from bronze). In the end the Krupp file was closed, with the words 'rien à faire' recorded in the margin of one of the documents.

The French government, unbeknown to itself, had substantially predetermined the outcome of the Franco-Prussian war. Funds for artillery re-equipment, in any event, would have been hard to come by. With 113 million francs earmarked for production of the Chassepôt, the government had asked the Chambers for 13 million to improve the artillery. A mere 2.5 million were forthcoming. The conservatism of the French military establishment which Napoleon could break down only on occasion, and the cheese-paring of the legislature which he could no longer defeat, combined to allow the Germans to enter the war with a decisive artillery superiority. This was the main factor which restored the tactical (and thus strategic) advantage of the attack as against French defensive strategy based in part on the superior range and fire-power of the Chassepôt.

In fact, how to strengthen the effectiveness of attack had been at the core of Moltke's tactical thinking. Impressed with the strength of the new infantry weapons in the defence of well-sited positions, he developed the tactic of seizing such positions when possible, to deny them to the enemy, and of by-passing or outflanking them if in hostile hands. A direct attack, where unavoidable, was to be launched only after extensive artillery preparation. Artillery, therefore, contrary to the tactics employed at Sadowa, must be not only highly mobile but positioned with the front-line troops. As against these views French tactical thinking, as befitted the possessors of Chassepôt and *mitrailleuse*, remained primarily defensive.

The war of 1870 at least in its first crucial weeks, turned essentially into a duel between M. Chassepôt and Messrs Krupp, with each of the major engagements following the same tactical pattern. According to a contemporary German observer, the needle-gun, the star of Sadowa, made no significant contribution. Fighting was either at close range with the bayonet or from a distance with artillery. The middle ground was dominated by Chassepôt and *mitrailleuse*. Time and again French infantry, entrenched in well-sited hill positions and using its Chassepôt rifles with devastating effect, beat off German charges whether of infantry or cavalry. Then, with greater or lesser delay, highly mobile German field artillery, outranging the Chassepôts, would appear and mercilessly pound the helpless French infantry from surrounding hill positions. After which the demoralized and, by this time, usually outflanked French troops would be driven from their positions at the point of the bayonet. Time and again, Moltke's forces would carry out his favourite pincer operations with artillery bombardment as an essential tactical preparation. The ubiquitous Prussian field artillery has been described by the historian of the war as 'the greatest tactical surprise of the Franco-Prussian war'. Napoleon himself, after the battle of Sedan, congratulated the Germans on the performance of their artillery.

The impact on Europe of the fall of the hitherto all but invincible French army – even the Germans had entered the war with considerable trepidation – was overwhelming. Lebœuf, on the eve of the war, had announced that the French army was ready. Ready, indeed, it had been to fight another campaign like the North Italian, against an opponent organized and equipped like itself. What neither Napoleon's professionals nor the subsequent armies of National Defence were able to withstand was a numerically superior mass army based on a nation in arms, guided in its movements by a General Staff trained by Moltke and armed with the guns forged by Krupp. The science of war, as the Prussians revealed to Europe, had advanced since the days of Sevastopol. The victors of Fort Malakoff and Solferino were no longer a match for those of Sadowa. Yet neither the Germans' superior staff-work nor their tactically superior weapons wholly explain the French collapse. The view, at any rate, was widespread at the time that other, intangible factors had played a part. The great chemist Berthelot, for instance, told one of the Goncourt brothers:

No, it is not so much the superiority of their artillery, it is something totally different and I will explain it to you. This is how matters are: if the Chief of the Prussian General Staff has received an order for an Army Corps to advance to a certain point by a certain time, he takes his maps, studies the country, the terrain, calculates the time a corps will need to cover a certain distance. . . . *Our* staff officer does nothing of the sort; in the evening, he follows his amusements; next morning, he presents himself on the field of battle and enquires whether the troops have arrived and which is the best place for an attack. It has been like that since the start of the campaign and this, I repeat, is the cause of our defeats.

As Berthelot rightly saw, the war was a clash of two different concepts of warfare.

The lesson for Europe appeared to be that in an industrial age it was only a mass army, professionally trained and directed and enjoying the benefit of every technological advantage, that could hope, in future, to be successful in a major war. Specialist training, the expertise of the often middle-class artilleryman, bridge-builder or railway engineer, would henceforth count for more than the dash of the cavalry officer or the *débrouillage* of the intrepid *troupier*. Romance and chivalry had – together with the romantic age – departed from serious warfare. At best, older aristocratic military virtues would now have to be fused with 'middle-class' organization, precision and attention to detail.

In countries with mixed social systems cavalry, now a military anachronism, would continue to hold its own for purely social or decorative reasons. The British army in particular, secure behind its moat and rooted in a stable social system, resisted the forces of change. At Majuba Hill, in the Boer War, even in Flanders, it would reveal the survival of the mentality of the Alma and Balaclava. Not for it the lessons of Sedan.

Great Britain, in this respect at least, stood outside the continental cycle of change. Chastened by the Crimean experience, her policies, from the mid-sixties onwards, were turned effectively towards 'splendid isolation'. Her imperial destinies were drawing her more and more away from Europe – where, indeed, the 'British age' which was also the age of prosperity, was drawing to its close. British land wars of the future were expected to be colonial wars, requiring the services of neither a Roon, a Moltke nor a Krupp. England's Krupps were her Armstrongs and her Whitworths, the inventors, engineers and technologists who assured her naval supremacy. The thinking and planning, organization, inventiveness, engineering skills and industrial resources which in Prussia-Germany had gone into the building of a new army, were in Britain lavished on the Royal Navy. Britain's counterpart to Chassepôt and steel field-gun was the gun-turret, an invention which revolutionized naval warfare. The turret-battleship *Devastation*, completed in 1873, has been described as 'such a combination of all that was new as to justify for her the title of "first modern battleship"'. So long as Britannia had her *Devastation*, she could, with a clear conscience, retain her cavalry.

68 H.M.S. *Devastation* (1873), the 'first modern battleship'.

In the event, whether in Krupp gun or Chassepôt or in the battleship *Devastation*, the age of prosperity had left its mark. Never again would warfare be the leisurely pursuit of gentlemen at arms – nor the happy hunting ground of the soldier of fortune risen from the ranks. War, henceforth, would be a 'serious business', and something of a science, the united effort of an industrial society.

69 Part of the Tuileries, damaged during the fighting of the Paris Commune;
it had finally to be demolished.

War, throughout the period, had proved to be not incompatible with prosperity. The end of the era of prosperity is attributable, if at all, only indirectly and to a limited extent to the Franco-Prussian war and its aftermath. In fact, at the start of the year 1872 – following almost four years of what Disraeli described as 'a convulsion of prosperity' – the economic barometer of English commercial life seemed to observers to stand at 'set fair', with a rising tendency. According to the reading of all the sensitive City indicators, the monetary aspect had seldom been more satisfactory. Everything was upward 'and honestly, not fictitiously, upward'. Of course one never knew what sudden storm might come and depress everything but there were no signs just then of any such storm. The average rise of at least one-third in railway stocks due not to speculation but to a genuine increase of rail traffic, told in itself an astonishing tale of commercial activity. Money was easy with the bank rate at 3 per cent. Business was active. New speculations were not of such a magnitude as to create misgivings in any quarter. What businessmen said of 1872 was very similar to what they had said at the start of 1871: 'The prospect is most promising.'

Yet national prosperity, as the year advanced, produced some disquieting symptoms. The *Annual Register* for 1873 spoke in retrospect of

> ... the increased difficulty of living, the alarming rise of prices in the most common commodities of life, and the unequal struggles of the salaried middle classes to keep abreast of the wave of wealth which threatened to sink them while the battle raged between capital and labour: the claims of the latter being emphasized by the rapid and dangerous growth of strikes which was to attain before the close of the year the most threatening proportions.

Meanwhile, indifference seemed to be more and more the leading characteristic of the great body of the middle class. Political and social agitation failed to strike a spark out of them, with any real flame in it. 'Only on the Prince's illness did the national pulse give evidence of life in any direction, save the making of money.'

In Great Britain at any rate, the year 1873 proved 'generally prosperous and tranquil'. But there had been tremors in several foreign countries. Reaction after a period of excessive speculation had produced serious embarrassment on the stock exchanges of Berlin and Frankfurt. At Vienna, the difficulties had amounted to a panic. In the autumn, a still graver crisis hit the USA. There were a number of failures among banks which had commanded general confidence. The cause of the crisis was seen as 'the investment in railway construction of an undue proportion of capital'. The short-term consequences were alarming: all banks virtually suspended payments. And, although the immediate crisis soon passed, 'every kind of enterprise was seriously discouraged, and the interruption of trade and the diminution of the demand for labour threatened to cause much distress during the winter'. The effect in Great Britain of these foreign upsets had been violent fluctuations in the bank rate, which ranged between 3 and 8 per cent. 'Trade in general continued moderately active,' the *Annual Register* reported, 'although the rate of increase was diminished.'

In 1874, economic life in Britain registered the first serious effects of the world-wide change in the economic climate. 'In the coal and iron trade . . . strikes occurred in consequence of the reduction in wages which began early this year after the long period of inflation.' Since the autumn of 1871, wage increases had been constant, varying in different districts from 50 to 86 per cent. Early in 1874, a change set in. The inflated price of coal in the preceding year had rapidly limited consumption. Iron, for the same reason, had been in short demand. Employers, faced with this situation, attempted to save by cutting wages. The men, who had enjoyed exceptionally high wages, found themselves faced with reductions of 10, 15 and, in some regions, 20 per cent. The numerous local strikes which ensued, according to the *Annual Register*, were 'not of a formidable character', and in every case it was the employer who proved substantially victorious. What contemporaries did not at once perceive was that the economic upsets of 1873–74 marked the end of an era, the passing of the prosperity that had opened with the great gold discoveries more than twenty years before. Later, 'Black Friday' (9 May 1873), the day the German exchanges broke, was said (with some exaggeration) to have impressed itself on the financial world as Cannae did on the Romans or Kossovo Polje on the Serbs. Even the House of Krupp, the biggest industrial enterprise in Europe, was almost ruined by the crash. Not only was Alfred Krupp obliged to lay off some 1,800 workmen (out of a total work force of about 11,500), but in 1874 financial difficulties forced him to pledge the entire property of the undertaking to the hated banks in return for a loan of 30 million marks and, worse still, to accept a representative of the banks to act as finance controller of the firm.

The immediate crisis, in the view of contemporaries, was the result of over-speculation and sudden loss of confidence. Yet similar crises, in 1857 and again ten years later, had been successfully surmounted. The fact that no real recovery followed the collapse of 1873 was due to underlying 'structural' causes. While the great boom was at its height, there had developed a vast and seemingly inexhaustible demand for rails, engines, steamships and machinery of every kind – and with it for the basic materials, coal, iron and steel. With generally rising prices, capacity had been expanded at an unprecedented rate. Now, most major countries had completed their building programme at least for the time being – in Russia, for example, the first peak period of railway construction lasted from 1868 to 1874 – and there was a sharp and fairly sudden contraction of demand. The result was over-capacity. The world's forges were capable in 1873 of producing 2.5 million tons of rails, but the actual demand reached no more than one-fifth of that amount. A slump in prices was the inevitable consequence. That of rails, for instance, fell by almost two-thirds between 1872 and 1881.

The drastic fall in the price of industrial products coincided with another depressive influence. New railway construction overseas had opened up vast virgin lands in North and South America and Australia, producing grain at a cost which European agriculture found it difficult to match. Thanks to bigger and faster vessels, aided in the case of Australia by the cutting of the Suez Canal, cheap grain began to pour into the major European ports. At the same time, railway construction had made possible large-scale exportation of grain from Russia's Black Earth zone. In 1865, the railway had reached Odessa, Russia's major grain port. Russian grain, produced in part by subsistence farming, was added to overseas competition. In consequence, agricultural prosperity collapsed almost simultaneously with industrial prices. For several decades, agriculture remained a depressed industry.

With the disappearance of a prosperous agriculture, moreover, the market contracted further for both consumer and capital goods. The fall in demand for the products of industry combined with agricultural depression to reverse the long-term economic trend inaugurated by the mid-century gold finds. But, like the growth of prosperity, its decline also was somewhat uneven. France, perhaps surprisingly in view of war and indemnities, achieved at least a temporary recovery. Not until the eighties would she too succumb finally to the prevailing economic stagnation. Russia, too, having entered the age of prosperity with a time-lag of several years, continued to prosper until the early eighties. Nor, in general, were all sectors of the population affected in equal degree by the onset of the 'Great Depression'. Since prices on the whole fell faster than wages, real wages, everywhere, rose – at any rate for the fully employed. However, notwithstanding limited exceptions, the rate of growth in the major countries underwent a drastic decline by comparison with the previous period.

The indirect effects of the 'Great Depression' were far-reaching. Together with prosperity disappeared many of the manifestations to which it had given rise. Among the first casualties was the system of free trade which had made a notable contribution to the prosperity of the fifties and sixties. Some economic units, it is true, had become larger with national consolidation. Nevertheless, the area of free, or relatively free, trade in Europe was drastically reduced. In the face of intense competition, often in shrinking markets, the organization of economic pressure groups proceeded apace, both in agriculture and industry. Everywhere governments, yielding to their pressures, introduced protective tariffs. Moreover, with the change in the economic climate, the widespread belief in the virtues of free trade declined sharply. Before long, the new protectionist and neo-mercantilist thinking merged into the imperialist philosophies of the eighties and nineties. The gospel of Adam Smith, so recently a panacea for many of the world's ills, could henceforth claim few adherents.

Together with free trade, there disappeared into limbo the philosophy of *laissez-faire*, the faith in 'rugged individualism', the ethic of Samuel Smiles. Economic recession underlined – what even in the age of prosperity had become clear to thoughtful contemporaries – that Smiles's gospel had been based on absurdly optimistic premises. As educated men and women were made increasingly aware – through social investigation and socialist propaganda – of the prevalence of widespread poverty and destitution, the complacent doctrine that hard

70 *Applicants for admission to a casual ward*, painted by Sir Luke Fildes in 1874 at the height of the 'Great Depression'.

work and frugality were the cure both for individual problems and for social ills lost credibility and support. Clearly, masses of people everywhere were prevented by social conditions from ever reaching the Smilesian starting-line. Recession – the rise in real wages notwithstanding – sharpened people's sensitivity to the widespread poverty the earlier age had often conveniently glossed over or treated as an evil, either temporary or self-inflicted.

The philosophy of entrepreneurial individualism, as propagated by Smiles, Spencer, or Bright, fell into growing disfavour with the realization of the need to extend state intervention to alleviate social ills. Workers everywhere were strengthening their unions in line with the general trend towards the emergence of stronger economic pressure groups. Not only was their philosophy predominantly collectivist, but in many instances they advocated state intervention in industry. Among middle-class intellectuals collectivist ideas, for somewhat different reasons, were gaining further ground at the expense of individualism and *laissez-faire*. The latter now came to be stigmatized as selfish, cruel and heartless. Even a champion of indi-

167

vidual freedom like John Stuart Mill became a convert to socialism. The intellectual and moral atmosphere of Europe was in process of transformation. It was the new economic climate as much as the teaching of Marx and Engels (which, however, gained in persuasiveness through the experience of the depression) that lay at the root of the change.

Liberalism, dead (or almost) in economics, obsolescent (at least in its classical form) as a social philosophy, was losing ground also in the political sphere. With the onset of the depression, the political affiliations more particularly of the once-liberal bourgeoisie underwent a change. One reason was a broad change of mood. The middle classes, outgoing, forward-looking, self-assured and expansionist while prosperity lasted, became self-centred, restrictionist and conservative once wholesale prices began to fall. Everywhere, the defence of narrow sectional concerns became a political preoccupation. The experience of the Paris Commune, moreover, suggested to the bulk of the industrial middle classes the prudence of an alignment with the conservative forces in society. So, indeed, did the urgent desire for bounties from the state in the shape of tariffs, government orders and subsidies. Commercial interests, together with some members of the liberal professions, alone remained faithful to earlier liberal philosophies, of which they happened also to be among the major beneficiaries. Everywhere, though less so in Great Britain than elsewhere, the bulk of the middle classes turned conservative.

At the same time the petty bourgeoisie of artisans, small shopkeepers and employees was turning to anti-capitalism, frequently in an anti-Semitic guise. Whereas the age of prosperity had seen the removal of residual Jewish disabilities, depression enabled demagogues from the Moskva to the Seine to direct anti-capitalist resentment into anti-Jewish channels. The revolt of the 'small man' against industrialization thus assumed new and increasingly illiberal forms. Capitalism, source of the 'economic miracle' of the fifties and sixties, had, indeed, been opposed – ineffectually – even in the age of prosperity by small traders, artisans, and hand-loom weavers, social groups whose interests it had harmed. In face of the 'miracle' their protest, though sometimes taken up for interested reasons by upper-class conservatives, had made little headway. Now, however, capitalism had become questionable in the eyes of many who had once admired its achievements. The evils of unbridled speculation appeared more glaring, the ruin of the unwary small investor or struggling artisan more shocking, when no longer matched by at least some expectation of future well-being for all. In the changed circumstances the social and human price exacted by the capitalist system was considered by many too high.

The growing disenchantment engendered by the Great Depression found its symbolical cultural and artistic expression in the new-found popularity of Richard Wagner's *Ring*. So long as prosperity lasted, the impact of Wagner's 'music of the future' had been slight. The depression, together with the accompanying change of mood, secured for his work a hitherto unsuspected resonance among Europe's upper classes. Powerful rulers like William II and Nicholas II became passionate 'Wagnerians'. Members of Europe's cultural élite flocked to the shrine newly opened in Bayreuth. The 'Master's' work, whatever its artistic merits, struck a chord in many hearts. While the anti-materialist symbolism of the *Rheingold* and the heroism of Siegfried satisfied the cravings of intellectuals, the cosmic pessimism of *Götterdämmerung* reflected a widespread mood (induced largely by falling wholesale prices) in the European bourgeoisie. It was, moreover, in keeping with the new mood that the cultural centre of gravity in Europe should (at least for a time) shift from Offenbach's Paris to gloomy Germanic Bayreuth. As for Paris itself, its intellectual climate changed under the impact of the Commune. Prominent among the 'best-sellers' of the depression were the harsh, accusing, naturalistic works of Zola (*L'Assommoir* – which established his reputation – 1878; *Nana* 1880; *Germinal* 1885). The gentler realism and satire of works like *Madame Bovary* had gone the way of prosperity and free trade, of *laissez-faire*, individualism and general liberal attitudes.

Again, some basic tenets of the age of prosperity, though they did indeed outlast it, underwent a significant change. The doctrine of evolution, once the centre-piece of Spencer's optimistic moral philosophy, became divorced from the liberal world view it had hitherto helped to sustain. The age of the Great Depression was also that of the delayed impact of Nietzsche's Zarathustra, of 'superman' and the 'revaluation of values'. Nietzsche's gospel was a Germanized version of the 'survival of the fittest', transposed into a new amoral and anti-bourgeois medium. According to Nietzsche, the man of the future would (and should) not be the successful scientist, inventor, engineer or businessman but the amoral, warlike 'blond beast'. His future 'biological' élite was not the product of a rational and enlightened age; it was a horde of intuitive and irrational Siegfrieds – and possibly Brunhildes, of whom, however, Nietzsche had less to say. The depression, with its reaction against the principles of emancipation, marked a setback also for feminist ideas. There would be no direct successors to George Sand, George Eliot and Florence Nightingale. (Bertha von Suttner, Beatrice Webb and the Suffragettes belong essentially to a subsequent generation.)

In the guise of social Darwinism, the age of prosperity had itself contributed to a new view of international relations. The Franco-Prussian war was the first international conflict widely interpreted in essentially Darwinist terms. It was held that the 'fittest' (the uncorrupted Germans) had triumphed over the 'unfit' (the corrupt and frivolous French). Success, moreover, had in fact demonstrated superior fitness. The lengths to which biological analogy could be carried in the discussion of international relations had already been revealed to the world in the botanist and ichthyologist Danilevsky's *Russia and Europe*. Yet during much of the age of prosperity, beginnings like these had been counteracted by an essentially liberal, that is internationalist, approach to relations among nations. With the retreat from bourgeois liberalism and its partial restraint on national excesses, the future increasingly would belong to the protagonists of a 'Darwinian' militarism, of 'blood and iron', and the *sacro egoismo* of nations. In a different sphere the age to a growing extent would be influenced by the apostles of a dehumanized dialectic of international class conflict. The decline of the liberal ethic, consequent on the onset of depression, would in retrospect give a new and sinister significance to such products of the previous age as Roon's reformed army, Moltke's General Staff and the 'crowning mercy' of Sedan. God, it was clear, had looked with favour on the 'nation in arms', the bigger battalions, and the steel-barrelled field-guns of the House of Krupp.

And yet as, paradoxically, the age of prosperity had also been an age of war, so – double paradox – the age of the Great Depression would be an era of unbroken peace. Except for the Russo-Turkish war, belated product of the earlier period and, in any case, not a conflict between major powers, no major wars occurred between 1871 and the mid-nineties, when the long depression began at last to lift. Together with prosperity and its varied concomitants, war too had disappeared. The peace, often attributed to the ascendancy of Germany and the diplomacy of Bismarck, survived at any rate the

71 The cover of *Germinal*, expressing the shift from Flaubert's gentler psychological realism to Zola's harsh accusing naturalism.

latter. If the 'scramble for Africa' and other non-European territories distracted the attention of the powers, it also provided more than once a possible occasion for war. Yet neither the Penjdeh incident nor Fashoda, neither Korea nor Morocco, terminated in armed conflict. Bismarck, in the age of the Great Depression, became a (satisfied) near-pacifist, as did Alexander III of Russia. French dreams of *revanche* were quietly shelved – to all appearances indefinitely. With even the Poles quiescent, crusades and liberating missions had lost their appeal, except for small numbers of Russians. While governments, taught by recent experience, were prudently preparing the means of technological warfare, their diplomatic strategies remained essentially defensive. As after Waterloo, they were becoming once more the prudent custodians of (greatly increased) resources. As after Waterloo, moreover, they were once again preoccupied primarily with questions of internal security. The age of Bismarck – that is, the age of the

Great Depression – was, in important respects, a replica of that of Metternich and Nicholas I. Thus, in the international sphere as in the domestic, the passing of prosperity marked a significant break.

Perhaps the most lasting legacy of the age of prosperity – a legacy that would shape the outlook and affect the conduct of individuals and governments, of businessmen and soldiers, of teachers in schools and universities – was the wide diffusion of a residual positivism, a belief in rational processes and scientific method. The new science, indeed, would lack some of the seeming certainties of the old. The trust in counting and weighing, however, in observing, measuring and quantifying remained. So did the craving for material progress, belief in the principle of utility, the 'greatest happiness of the greatest number'. The faith in education held by the pioneers of the age of prosperity gained in strength. Universal secular education and, even more, developing technical education helped further to disseminate such ideas. Perhaps the single most representative monument to the age of prosperity is the great South Kensington complex in London, with its varied educational institutions, developed, appropriately, on ground bought with the proceeds of the Great Exhibition of 1851. It was here that the most significant aspects of the spirit of prosperity would, in due course, be preserved.

Despite determined attacks, the ideas represented by the educational complex of South Kensington would never wholly yield to those expressed by Bayreuth. Soviet man and society, the 'American Way of Life', perhaps 'Europe of the Nine', are their lasting memorial.

72 A board-school for girls in 1876.

73 (*Above*) The Prince Consort Gallery in the Victoria and Albert Museum, London.

SELECT BIBLIOGRAPHY

I PORTRAIT OF AN AGE
A. Briggs, *Victorian People* (New York 1955).
W. L. Burn, *The Age of Equipoise* (London 1964).

II THE ECONOMICS OF PROSPERITY
C. Beattie, *Ferdinand de Lesseps* (London 1956).
R. E. Cameron, *France and the Economic Development of Europe 1800–1914* (Princeton, N.J. 1961).
C. M. Cipolla (ed.), *The Industrial Revolution* (London 1973).
E. Corti, *The Reign of the House of Rothschild* (London 1928).
D. A. Farnie, *East and West of Suez* (Oxford 1969).
J. Faucher (ed.), *Vierteljahrsschrift für Volkswirthschaft und Kulturgeschichte*, Band XXXI (Berlin 1871).
B. Gille, *Histoire de la Maison Rothschild* (Geneva 1965–67).
H. Heaton, *Economic History of Europe* (New York 1963).
W. O. Henderson, *The Industrialization of Europe 1780–1914* (London 1969).
E. J. Hobsbawm, *Industry and Empire* (London 1968).
P. A. Khromov, *Ekonomicheskoe razvitie Rossii v XIX–XX vekakh* (Moscow 1950).
C. von Klass, *Krupps* (London 1954).
D. S. Landes, *The Unbound Prometheus: Technological Change and Industrial Development in Western Europe from 1750 to the Present* (Cambridge 1969).
Ch. Morazé, *Les Bourgeois Conquérants* (Paris 1957).
D. H. Pinkney, *Napoleon III and the Re-building of Paris* (Princeton, N.J. 1958).
L. Reybaud, *Le Fer et la Houille* (Paris 1874).
A. T. Wilson, *The Suez Canal* (London 1933).

III THE PHILOSOPHY OF PROSPERITY AND ITS CRITICS
W. Bagehot, *Physics and Politics* (5th edn London 1879).
J. Barzun, *Darwin, Marx, Wagner* (New York 1958).
M. Burckhardt (ed.), *Jacob Burckhardt, Briefe* V (Basle-Stuttgart 1963).
R. Hofstadter, *Social Darwinism in American Thought* (Boston, Mass. 1955).
G. Lukács, *Die Zerstörung der Vernunft* (Berlin 1962).
T. Mackay (ed.), *The Autobiography of Samuel Smiles* (London 1905).
G. Masur, *Prophets of Yesterday* (London 1963).
W. M. Simon, *European Positivism in the Nineteenth Century* (Ithaca, N.Y. 1963).
S. Smiles, *Self-Help* (London 1859; many reprints, 1860 to 1958).

IV THE CULTURE OF PROSPERITY AND ITS CRITICS
M. Arnold, *Culture and Anarchy* (Cambridge 1935).
R. Bellet, *Presse et Journalisme sous le Second Empire* (Paris 1967).
J. M. & B. Chapman, *Baron Haussmann* (London 1957).
E. Friedell, *Kulturgeschichte der Neuzeit* III (Munich 1931).
R. Hamann & J. Hermand, *Gründerzeit* (Berlin 1969).
N. Pevsner, 'Art and Architecture' in J. P. T. Bury (ed.), *The New Cambridge Modern History*, vol. x (Cambridge 1960).
N. Ponente, *The Structures of the Modern World 1850–1900* (Geneva 1965).
J. Pudney, *The Thomas Cook Story* (London 1953).

E. Saunders, *The Age of Worth, Couturier to the Empress Eugénie* (London 1954).
A. Trollope, *An Autobiography* (London 1950).
H. Vanier, *La Mode et ses Métiers* (Paris 1960).
M. Zimmermann, *Die Gartenlaube als Dokument ihrer Zeit* (Munich 1963).

V THE POLITICS OF PROSPERITY
E. N. Anderson, *The Social and Political Conflict in Prussia 1858–1864* (Lincoln, Neb. 1954).
A. Briggs, *Victorian People* (New York 1955).
W. L. Burn, *The Age of Equipoise* (London 1964).
J. P. T. Bury, *Napoleon III and the Second Empire* (London 1964).
E. Feder (ed.), *Bismarcks grosses Spiel. Die geheimen Tagebücher Ludwig Bambergers* (Frankfurt a.M. 1932).
T. S. Hamerow, *Restoration, Revolution, Reaction: Economics and Politics in Germany, 1815–1871* (Princeton, N.J. 1958).
— *The Social Foundations of German Unification 1858–1871* (Princeton, N.J. 1969).
O. Pflanze, *Bismarck and the Development of Germany* (Princeton, N.J. 1963).
Politische Correspondenz, *Die innere Politik der Preussischen Regierung von 1862 bis 1866* (Berlin 1866).
W. H. C. Smith, *Napoleon III* (London 1972).
J. Vincent, *The Foundation of the Liberal Party 1857–1868* (London 1966).
T. Zeldin, *The Political System of Napoleon III* (London 1958).

VI ATTITUDES TO MILITARISM AND WAR
E. N. Anderson, *The Social and Political Conflict in Prussia, 1858–1864* (Lincoln, Neb. 1954).
W. Bagehot, *Physics and Politics* (5th edn London 1879).
A. Briggs, *Victorian People* (New York 1955).
J. Burckhardt, *Welthistorische Betrachtungen* (Leipzig 1935).
J. Casevitz, *Une Loi manquée: la Loi Niel (1866–1868)* (Rennes 1959).
C. Kingsley, *His Letters and Memories of his Life* edited by his wife (London 1908).

G. Ritter, *Staatskunst und Kriegshandwerk* I (Munich 1965).
J. Ruskin, *The Crown of Wild Olive* (Works, vol. XVIII) (London 1905).

VII THE NEW DIPLOMACY
W. E. Mosse, *The European Powers and the German Question 1848–1871* (New York 1969).
O. Pflanze, *Bismarck and the Development of Germany* (Princeton, N.J. 1963).
W. H. C. Smith, *Napoleon III* (London 1972).

VIII ARMIES AND SOCIETIES
E. N. Anderson, *The Social and Political Conflict in Prussia 1858–1864* (Lincoln, Neb. 1954).
G. Craig, *The Politics of the Prussian Army, 1640–1945* (Oxford 1955).
K. Demeter, *The Prussian Officer Corps* (London 1965).
B. D. Gooch, *The New Bonapartist Generals in the Crimean War* (The Hague 1959).
M. Howard, *The Franco-Prussian War* (London 1962).
G. Ritter, *Staatskunst und Kriegshandwerk* I (Munich 1965).
C. Woodham-Smith, *Florence Nightingale 1820–1910* (London 1950).
— *The Reason Why* (London 1953).

IX THE SINEWS OF WAR
G. A. Craig, *The Battle of Königgrätz* (London 1965).
M. Howard, *The Franco-Prussian War* (London 1962).
C. von Klass, *Krupps* (London 1954).
M. Lewis, 'Armed Forces and the Art of War: Navies'; and
B. H. Liddell-Hart, 'Armed forces and the Art of War' both in J. P. T. Bury (ed.), *The New Cambridge Modern History*, vol. X (Cambridge 1960).

X EUROPE WITHOUT PROSPERITY
H. Rosenberg, *Grosse Depression und Bismarckzeit* (Berlin 1967).

INDEX

177

ACKNOWLEDGMENTS

Her Majesty the Queen, 25; Bibliothèque Historique de la Ville de Paris, 12; Bibliothèque Nationale, Paris, 48; British Library, 3, 7, 16, 17, 29, 35, 37, 44, 46, 47, 53, 61, 63, 64; British Museum Print Room, 1, 51; City Art Gallery, Manchester, 5; Clifton Society, 40; Dresden Gallery, 33; Mary Evans Picture Library, 67, 68; Governor and Company of the Bank of England, 6; Greater London Council, 31; Imperial War Museum, London, 59; Krupps, Essen, 14, 15; Louvre, 26, 34, 36; Mansell Collection, 72; Merksches Hausarchiv Darmstadt, 22; Musée Carnavalet, Paris, 49; Musée Condé, Chantilly, 66; Museo del Risorgimento, Turin, 59; Nationalbibliothek, Vienna, 30; National Portrait Gallery, London, 20, 21, 48, 58; Parker Gallery, London, 60; Pierpont Morgan Library, 23; Radio Times Hulton Picture Library, 50; Roger-Viollet, Paris, 13, 24; Royal College of Surgeons of England, 19; Royal Holloway College, 8, 70; St Bride Printing Library, 42; Edwin Smith, 32; Staatsbibliothek Berlin, 27, 28, 62, 65; Trades Union Congress, London, 18; Victoria and Albert Museum, London, 2, 39, 41, 69, 73.